Absolutely

JOANNA
LUMLEY

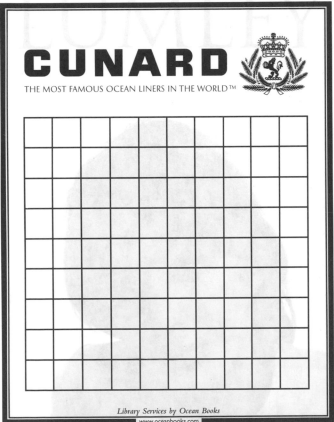

CUNARD
THE MOST FAMOUS OCEAN LINERS IN THE WORLD™

Absolutely

JOANNA LUMLEY

WEIDENFELD & NICOLSON

Contents

Out of India   10

Early Years   36

Make-up and Mini-skirts   48

And Introducing...   86

The Big Break   116

This is the Life   140

Being Fabulous   178

As Good as it Gets   202

From Here to Kingdom Come   212

My Family   246

The Gurkhas   260

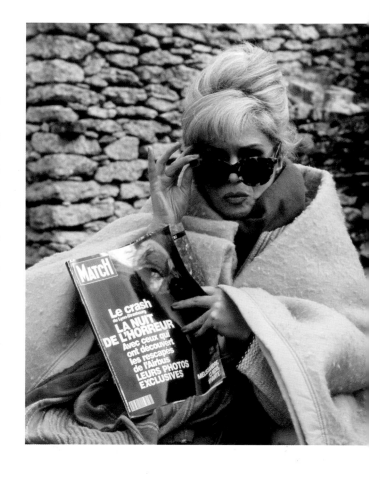

Half title: *Aged twenty in trendy grandpa vest.
Lower eyelashes drawn on heavily. Trying to make
my shoulders look narrower.*

Title page left: *In a Zandra Rhodes dress on
Patrick Lichfield's motorbike. Rather shiny tights
make the legs look like sausages.*

Title page right: *As Purdey in the* New Avengers.
*An early publicity shot with the Purdey haircut
unveiled.*

Left: *With Eric and Ernie when I appeared in their
show. The theme was The Twenties and I had to
sing 'Thoroughly Modern Millie.'*

Above: *Patsy's dreadful circulation meant that she
was freezing cold even in the South of France and
had to resort to rugs and magazines to keep the blood
travelling round her raddled body.*

Introduction

I have hoarded things all my life; letters and lamp-stands, pencils and chairs, bales of cloth and used wrapping paper. I can't help it and I can't stop. I have in some way hoarded my very life, as there is in every room of our hugely overcrowded house something from long ago which reminds me of being a child or a lumpy teenager, or even a time before I was born when my parents and grandparents travelled with their regiments or duties around the Far East, Tibet and India. This amassing of memories serves me well, yet slows me down; nothing can be discarded without a 'chance to see again', as the BBC would put it, a repeat performance of its original role, yellowed and cracked now with time but bringing into sharp focus days and words and clothes from another age.

However, nothing comes close to the power of photographs in evoking memories. My mother Beatrice, from whom I have inherited the hoarding bug (although mine is much more diluted than hers: she could actually feel sorry for a spoon or 'give a kind home' to a three-legged table) saved everything; pieces of string, abandoned lids, my sister's drawings and every magazine or newspaper she could lay hands on in which I appeared as a model. These she kept in old suitcases, dangling with labels saying 'Not Wanted On Voyage' or 'Barclay's Bank Nairobi' or 'Singapore'. Mixed with these relics of the time, when fashionable Britain was in the grip of mini-skirts and wigs, were letters and postcards from days before the days I could remember: and albums, envelopes and files of photographs. When these were added to the really colossal amount of press cuttings, publicity stills, reviews, old school reports and articles which I had amassed through the years, now cunningly concealed in bland-looking boxes and folders and trunks, it would be fair to say that it was an awe-inspiring collection.

Far from making it easier to have such a treasure trove to dig into to prepare this book, it has made it fifty times harder. For some reason

Playing Desdemona with Michael Levete as Othello for the Old Harrovian Players. The costumes were on loan from the Royal Shakespeare Company. The character in front of the curtains is Richard Curtis, yet to leave school and begin his exciting and extraordinary career. Comic Relief was not yet born.

I want to show you, dear reader, everything I have: like an exhibitionist, or, to be frank, like a crashing bore, I want to say 'Oh look at this! We were on location in Canada' or 'Do you see that hat? I made it myself from a lampshade'. As my life stretches away behind me I find that I can still see the end of the tail as it winds back through films and campaigns, modelling trips and school plays, lost front teeth and my own baby boy. So the hardest bit has been what to choose and what to let drift; what might ring a bell in your own memory and what is honestly only there because I thought I looked nice in that dress.

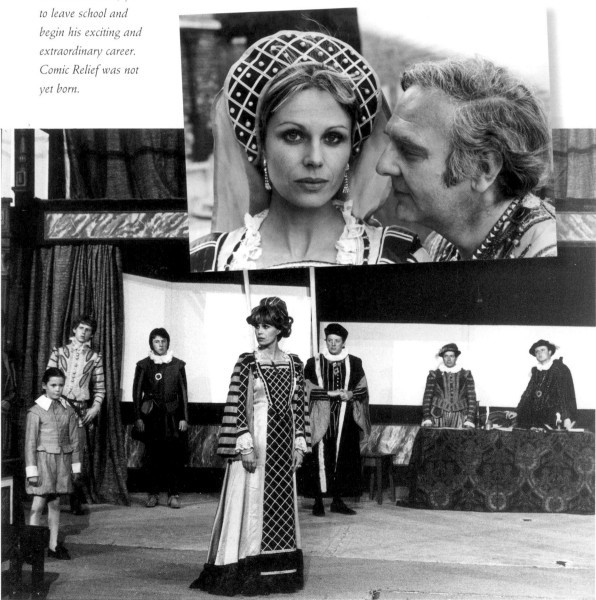

I have hoarded up memories too: to recall the names of girls in my class at school, of make-up artists and directors, I put my brain into slow-trawl and usually I come up with an identity. But memory can play fearful tricks, and I am stunned to find that I cannot remember the dates of any work I did after *Sapphire and Steel*. Perhaps my brain was marooned along with those valiant space travellers in an abandoned petrol station, slowly circling the cosmos, Sapphire in her blue dress and Steel still inhabiting the handsome form of the erstwhile Illya Kuryakin; for as actors we are all replaceable, memorable for a while if we are lucky, then fading to black as the world spins towards another goal. How I hate forgetting the people I have been so close to; in our world we are like a travelling circus troupe, trapeze artists, wholly reliant on each other, moving on from town to town, smiling and striking a pose even when there are only three men and a dog in the audience, packing our shabby cases in our tiny, dirty changing rooms, and moving on, moving on. Since I have played Broadway her old showbiz tunes rattle round my head more often, and 42nd street is a reality now, where there's no business like show business and plays open and shut like a butterfly's wings. We are guaranteed nothing, and that is the reason I chased after the caravans as they rumbled out of town; nothing is certain and every day is new. I find that rather thrilling.

Each picture I have chosen brings with it, like a gauze cloak, its own insistent story. Even a knitting pattern photograph has its own dignity (or actually its own sweat-inducing reality of how things were in 1965). My life has been long and eventful: sometimes, like the character Zelig from the Woody Allen film, I seem to have appeared everywhere and in everything. The far-away childhood and the 'Angela Brazil' boarding schools lead on to becoming a model in the sixties, and a Bond girl: after that, an Avenging partner of John Steed and a victim of Dracula give way to Hedda Gabler and Oscar Wilde; and behind all this are the travel documentaries and journeys and family and friends, besides crashing about as Patsy in *Absolutely Fabulous*. How on earth can I cram all this into one book? Well, I think I have made a pretty good stab at it, and I have included everything that is important to me that I think will interest you. Although I have never been the subject of the programme *This Is Your Life* I have been a guest on the show many times: and it seems that This Is MY Life, specially prepared for you, but in a luxury edition, containing everything but nuts.

To get off to a flying start I want to begin before I was born, to explain a bit about where I come from and why I was there. I want you to be interested, charmed, amazed and amused. This book is for you.

Out of India

More than a hundred elephants and their
mahouts. You can tell which region the men
are from by the way they tie their turbans.
Each area has a slightly different look.
This photograph taken out of my paternal
grandfather's album makes me think it may
have been from the great Durbar of 1908, a
few years before the famous Delhi Durbar.
   'Durbar' means festivity/celebration/huge
event. Long ago it was commonplace for
elephants to be used rather in the same way
as horses were in the west, as beasts of burden
and haulage and panoply.

My mother's family, the Weirs.

In the days of the British Empire it was normal for people to be born in a distant land, to live, work and be married abroad and yet to think of Britain as 'home'. Home was where you went on leave, by ship, staying for about six months before returning to India, or the Far East or Africa, or to what were called the colonies. On both sides of my family India was home for several generations. They were all soldiers at some stage, but their principal employment was in the political or medical services. Today it is hard to imagine the way people travelled in those days: by slow and unreliable motorcars on bumpy roads, in horse-drawn carriages and

My great–grandfather was known in the family as GrandPat: his name was Colonel Patrick Weir of the Indian Medical Service: here he is seen in his dashing white uniform somewhere in the Central Provinces of India.

His son Leslie was my grandfather. He was born in Ghazipur in 1883 and joined the 5th Cavalry of the Indian army. He laid out a nine-hole golf course in Tibet, sent seeds from rare Himalayan plants to King George V and spoke twelve languages.

steam trains, on horseback or on foot, on board ships with spartan accommodation; and yet the journeys were made, the post got through and telegrams remained the most reliable way of sending urgent messages. To travel home took weeks, not hours. Most children used to be sent to England to be educated, and often didn't see their parents for three or four years. Husbands and wives got used to being apart for months at a time. It was a different world.

My mother's father, Leslie Weir, was a diplomat; his naturally friendly nature made him a trustworthy and welcome guest in countries that were suspicious of the outside world, countries like Tibet and Bhutan. As he always took the trouble to learn the language and know the local customs he was able to remain on the friendliest terms with everyone he met, from kings and prime ministers to porters and grooms. My mother's mother Thyra was Danish but had been born in New Zealand, where her father Christian Sommers had set up his life and family in the 19th century. She met Leslie while she was in Burma; my great-uncle Bart, her brother, was building a hospital there, and because he was a bachelor at the time Thyra went with him to run his household. My grandparents' wedding was quite small and without the usual complement of family guests and close friends, as Burma was a long way from India and New Zealand.

Granny Weir, Thyra Letitia Alexandra Sommers as she was before she married, was an actress through and through, although she only appeared in amateur dramatics in India.

When my grandparents married in Rangoon Hugh Gaitskell was one of their pageboys, the one sitting at Granny's feet. Her brother Bartholomew is standing behind her, with a balding head: he had been building a hospital in Burma and Thyra went to keep house for him.

Granny standing at the right with her riding crop over her shoulder appears to be instructing the unknown photographer as to the best angle. In the distance are some of the horses which the men had ridden to reach the picnic spot. The women would have come up in open horse-drawn carriages (although my mother used to tuck her skirt into trousers which she wore under her dress and ride astride to parties and picnics like this one).

I wish I could remember Grandpa: I did know him when I was tiny, and I sat on his lap when he visited us in Hong Kong, but I only have a small blurry photograph of that occasion. Everyone loved him; he died, too young, of leukaemia and is buried in Kenya which is where my grandparents went to live when he retired; 'home' wasn't

England to them as they had never lived there. My grandmother Thyra had a dashing personality, great artistic talent (and temperament) and immense personal charm. Theirs was a life of duty, travel and recreation. Duty led them to Persia and Sikkim, Bhutan, Kashmir and Tibet and all over India and the Middle East. My grandfather was what was called a Resident, a sort of mix of an ambassador, advisor and go-between. Often the places he visited or resided were off the beaten track, and British India was keen to know how things were in these distant outposts; whether the ruler was sympathetic to the British or to Russia, the other super-power looming in the north, or the Chinese in the east, always ready to move in to what they saw as their own recalcitrant territories. He gathered and gave information, made friends, officiated at functions, and often collected seeds of rare plants to send back to His Majesty King George V and to Kew Gardens. Grandpa and Granny Weir lived in Residencies, quite grand buildings that came with the job; theirs was an Edwardian lifestyle, with hard work interspersed with dinner parties and point-to-points, hunting, shooting and fishing, tennis and amateur dramatics.

They had two daughters: Joan Mary, a tall blonde blue-eyed beauty, crack shot, artist and breaker of hearts, and then, seven years later, my mother Beatrice, black haired and green-eyed, a brave and kind-hearted tomboy. Both were sent back to be schooled in England, and for the girls, being seven years apart in age, these were solitary sojourns. They were looked after in turn by kindly but ancient guardians and they communicated with their parents by letter, as no-one telephoned in those days, least of all schoolchildren. In faraway Himalayan countries there was no electricity, let alone telephones. When my aunt left school she returned to India to be with her parents, just as my mother was being sent off to be a boarder in a cold country unknown to her, where she was not allowed to see

Thyra cutting a dash on a hot day. Even in heat-waves or monsoons you were expected to dress properly, with petticoats and stockings, hat, gloves, and in this case a parasol.

other children in the holidays. She made her guardians' animals her friends, and from her I have inherited my love for all creatures great and small. Being at school she missed the great journeys her family made: my aunt Joan Mary used to send her drawings and descriptions of the extraordinary and exciting places they visited, notably Tibet and Bhutan. My mother, at school in Hampshire, would think of the pony she had left behind in Sikkim, and imagine their long trips on horse and foot with mules and yaks; and she would dream in Urdu, her first language, taught to her by her *ayah*, her Indian nursemaid. As soon as she left school she went back to rejoin her family in the great sub-continent she considered her home all her life.

POTALA
LHASA.

BEST WISHES FROM
LIEUT.-COLONEL AND MRS. LESLIE WEIR,
THE RESIDENCY,
GANGTOK, SIKKIM.

My grandparents' Christmas card. The Potala in Lhasa was the palace of successive Dalai Lamas before Tibet was invaded by the Chinese. In the 1930s Grandpa had become a close personal friend of the thirteenth Dalai Lama, the spiritual and political leader of Tibet; Granny was the first European woman to visit this majestic and secretive capital city.

Things haven't changed much; anywhere in the world this sort of formal photograph is familiar to this day. Carpets were often spread on the grass, making any lawn or courtyard into a grand outdoor salon. Granny always took her dogs with her on these long diplomatic journeys.

My father's family, the Lumleys.

My father, James Rutherford Lumley, was born in Lahore: his father, Charles Chester Lumley, was the son of a clergyman, William Faithfull Lumley, the chaplain of Chelmsford Prison; the family was large and money was fairly scarce. His great-grandfather was the splendidly named Adjutant-General to the Indian Army in 1798, Major-General Sir James Rutherford Lumley, and even though young Charles was brought up in England he decided to follow his ancestors to India to seek his fortune. I don't think it was a fortune, but it was a respectable and responsible job, running a big bank in western India, as it was before the creation of Pakistan. He met and married my grandmother, Ella Marion Young, in India and like my mother my father was sent home to school, seeing his parents only once in four years. He had three sisters, Rosa, Arabella and Isobel; when my grandfather retired from the bank the whole family left to live in England, but my father was to return to serve in the Indian Army as a Gurkha officer.

As I get older there are a thousand things I wish I had asked my parents. I never met my grandfather Charles: nor for that matter did my mother, as he died before she and my father met. I wonder what kind of a man he was: my aunts said he was a very gentle man, mild-mannered and humorous. I hardly knew my grandmother Ella either, but I have the beautiful little diamond necklace she wore on her wedding day; it was left to me by my aunt and I shall leave it in turn to the next generation. My latest resolution is to write who, when and where on the back of every photograph I have. It may take ages but as my own memory fades (not yet! but surely soon) it is the least I can do for my grandchildren. You think you will never forget an event, or that someone's face is too familiar or well-known to need identifying but I shall do it just in case. Memory is like smoke. You can see it clearly…and then it is gone, leaving not a trace behind.

My grandfather sits in the centre with the staff of the Bank of Bengal in Lahore. This must have been a day of celebration as they are wearing garlands of flowers; the blooms look like tuberoses and marigolds, maybe carnations. I love the custom of garlanding: men look extra-manly when decked out in blossom.

19

The status of Viceroy of India was sometimes considered to be even higher than the King's; the stupendous pageants and awe-inspiring ceremony that attended his every move were a feast for the eyes. Here in a photograph taken from my paternal grandfather's album the Viceroy Lord Curzon and Lady Curzon make sure their guests the Duke and Duchess of Connaught are comfortable in their howdah on the elephant on the right.

Daddy with some Gurkhas on the padang, *the parade ground, in Kuala Lumpur. There can seldom have been sharper creases on shorts.*

I never asked my father why he joined the Gurkhas. There were many other Indian regiments at the time. Like all who applied to become Gurkha officers you had to learn to speak Gurkhali first. You had to serve six months in another British regiment first (which one, Daddy? Why didn't I ask or make a note?) and then you were catapulted in at the deep end. Jimmy's first tour of duty was on the North West Frontier, with a hundred fighting-fit Nepali soldiers who thought nothing of running up sheer mountains with a full pack on their back. Daddy loved the Gurkhas completely: he loved their bravery and humour, their modesty and wicked sense of fun. As soldiers they had,

OBLIGATORY NEPALI SENTENCES

100 Sentences
that have occurred
in recent Obligatory Nepali Examinations
with translations
and
50 common Words
which recur in the examinations
but appear to be often unknown

by
Brigadier. R. G. Leonard,
O. B. E.

17. Dailo thunieko thiyo ani tala bata ragat bagdai aundai thiyo

The door shut and blood streamed out from below

19. Jahan sukai gaye pani gaun ma mareko manchhe matrai phela paren

Wherever I went I came across dead men only in the village

41. Tetikheri mero ghar khatkera ma Silkkim ma saryo

Then my house fell down and I moved to Sikkim

These rather gruesome phrases were important to learn for the Obligatory Nepali Examination: you had to pass to be allowed into a Gurkha regiment.

My father, very young. He had only just joined the regiment as a second-lieutenant.

The Gurkha soldier is never without his kukri; the legend is that, having been drawn from its sheath, it has to see blood before it goes back. Certainly it strikes terror into the hearts of anyone who has the misfortune to come up against it.

and have, no equals in the world and are feared, respected and loved by all who come into contact with them.

The Second World War had started when my parents met, in Srinagar where Grandpa Weir was Resident at the time; Jimmy would have been on leave. Srinagar, capital of Kashmir, is sublimely beautiful. Great lakes are surrounded by Himalayan mountains, kingfishers dip and flash in the water, huge plane trees, *chinars*, cast cooling shadows in the hot summer months; and the hard, snowy winters give way to spring with all the flowers of paradise bursting from the cold ground. On the lakes are houseboats, enormous moored wooden palaces reached by *shikaras*, little gondolas propelled by paddles shaped like hearts. No wonder people fell in love there; no wonder my parents spent their honeymoon there in 1941, on a houseboat moored on the Dal Lake. When Srinagar became too hot the British retreated to Gulmarg, an alpine resort reached only on foot or on horseback. High up in the pine forests were long wooden bungalows called 'huts'. Granny and Grandpa Weir had a hut up there; there were picnics and dances, golf tournaments and hill-walking to make a holiday complete and unforgettable. Now a road has been built up to Gulmarg and coaches filled with tourists make the slow steep journey upwards, to Nedou's Hotel and the Golf Course. There is a ski lift too; a changed and crowded place. Everywhere changes. The Buddhists say the only thing in life you can be absolutely certain of is change.

Jimmy was a very good horseman and often rode in point-to-points. Here he receives a handshake and a cup. Everyone had dogs in those days and when they rode out with their assorted hounds it was called a 'bobbery pack'.

My father sent an assortment of photographs to his mother in England, probably writing the details on the back of each picture, as this is my grandmother's hand. She stuck them all into an album which was eventually passed down to me.

SELF ON MY 7/8 CHARGER COLORADO

Lhasa
Tibet.

August 21st 1930

My darling Beatrice
This letter will I hope go by air so
it will have come a long journey – first on
coolys back all the way from here to the tra—
at Kalimpong Road Station. (where we met t
that day do you remember?)

Well, we have been here for a fortnight n
& I have met lots of lovely Tibetan ladies
wear wonderful silk   naturally sa
themselves with jewel   t
but as they wear so   loo
never run about or   for
wouldn't like that
important all the
real good walks or   t m

It is lovely here in a   pro
we stay for another month, which
shall do. only it will be cold going dow
Langtok Kenough Southern Tibet an
passes in October.   We

*Daddy dressed for
dinner at King's House
with the Templers in
Kuala Lumpur. He
was ADC to General,
later Field Marshal,
Sir Gerald Templer,
High Commissioner to
the Federated Malay
States.*

*Mummy in Hong Kong.
When we were there the
tallest building was four
stories high.*

*A letter from Granny to Beatrice, my mother, who was ten and at boarding school in England.
Granny describes a long visit to Lhasa; she and Mummy's elder sister Joan Mary made
wonderful drawings of all they saw, while my grandfather talked matters of state with the
thirteenth Dalai Lama. Mummy grew up to love mountains almost more than anything in her
life; she was at her happiest at the thought of a really gruelling trek.*

These were called Polyphotos: nowadays they would be called contact sheets. These were taken in England when we were on leave: I must have been a year and a half.

I was born in Kashmir, in Srinagar, on the first day of May in 1946. My sister Aelene had been born two years before in Abbottabad, in present day Pakistan, and she could speak a little Urdu when we left India for good in 1947 but I was too young to speak or remember anything from that time. We sailed home to Southampton on the *Franconia*, and then started the journeying to and from the Far East by ship; the *Windrush*, the *Empire Orwell*, the *Dilwara*. Each trip took about a month to reach Singapore, five weeks if you were going to Hong Kong. We washed in tin baths in sea water and showered with fresh water to rinse away the salt. Every day we had an orange to eat: we looked forward to the Suez Canal where a pilot would be brought out to the ship by motor launch, nimbly climbing aboard on a lowered ladder to steer us through the canal's narrow banks into the Mediterranean, or, if we were going east, into the Red Sea. For two years we lived in Hong Kong; for three years we were stationed in Kuala Lumpur, where the Emergency was at its height, with communist terrorists moving down the Malay Peninsula to be fought off and repulsed by the Gurkhas amongst other troops. Malaya became my home utterly; I loved the sultry tropical heat, the vivid colours of flowers and birds, the sudden black thunderstorms and scarlet sunsets. My sister and I walked

Sitting on Grandpa Weir's lap in Hong Kong. They came to visit us before setting off for Kenya where their house at Karen had just been built.

ARMY FORM B.155.

Embarkation of Military Families and Female Servants.

MEDICAL CERTIFICATE.

To be prepared in duplicate and completed by a Medical Practitioner within 3 days of date of embarkation, *vide* paras. 1169, 1170 and 1171 King's Regulations, 1940.

The Bearer, Wife of_____

of the_____Regiment, and_____Children have been inspected by me, and I find them free from infectious disease and in all respects medically fit for Embarkation.

The bearer was last
{ Inoculated with TAB on_____

{ Vaccinated on_____

Date at_____

_____ *Medical Practitioner.*

The age and sex of each child and the date on which each was last inoculated and vaccinated are to be stated on the other side.

No Officer's or Soldier's wife within three months of her approaching confinement is to be returned as medically fit for embarkation (para. 1170 King's Regulations, 1940).

Where it is not possible for inoculation to be carried out by a family's medical practitioner, the family should arrange for this to be done at the nearest Military Hospital. Travelling expenses incurred by a journey to the Military Hospital must be paid by the individual.

The form will be completed within three days of Embarkation, and ~~....~~ until handed over to the Movement Control Officer at the ~~....~~ cases where the certificate is dated more than ~~....~~ or individual will be re-exam~~....~~ Port of Embarkation, in ~~....~~

Both copies of this pap~~....~~ should be given personally ~~....~~ Troops.

(71148) 8482/2393 10m (P) 6/50 S.(P&L~~....~~

On board ship; my sister is in charge of someone else's baby in the foreground; I am sitting on some lap in the middle. We were going to Hong Kong and it looks hot and sweaty. The ships were without frills; deck quoits and games of canasta were the high spots for grown-ups. Children attended on-board schools but we were exempt as my father used to devise lessons for us of reading and writing.

Our hair was cut into neat cool pudding basins. We were always brown from swimming but no-one sunbathed in the tropical heat: only mad dogs went out in the midday sun, not English children. In later life I overtook my sister in height but here I am still shorter by half a head.

each day to the Army School; travel was restricted and during school holidays if we went to cooler parts of the country like Fraser's Hill we had to drive in an armed convoy.

We lived in an army bungalow on the edge of a little airstrip. The garden was non-existent when we arrived but in the three years we were there my father planted trees and flowers and made a lawn from the tough saw-toothed grass called *lalang*. Our lives followed ordered paths: school at 8 o'clock, before the heat of the day came slamming down, until midday; then walk home on a rough road made of great chunks of crystal quartz, like stepping over diamonds as big as the Ritz; a siesta after lunch, a walk to the tin mines with the dog; mucking about on the verandah or playing the wind-up gramophone until supper; then bath, reading, bed with the night sounds of the Malayan creatures clicking and croaking through the closed shutters in the velvet blackness.

We always had some sort of animals: Judy, our golden laughing dog, had been abandoned at the Officers' Mess on Christmas Eve so she came home to us for ever, and Kinky, our imperturbable and placid cat had been rescued from drowning by my mother while we were walking the dog. There was an iguana for a short time, and three ducklings bought in the market to ease the strain on their basket, stuffed so full with the anxious little feathery bodies, but although I prayed every night I never got a pony (I never actually saw a pony in Malaya; and I only ever saw three sheep, and they looked like goats). A home without an animal was unthinkable.

The guinea pigs, Sammy and Michael, we kept on a balcony in the Hong Kong flat; by the time we got to Malaya we had Judy, our golden stray dog, and cats, of whom Kinky was the most senior. A friend's budgie on my head reminds me of the Egyptian bird-god Horus.

Daddy taught us to swim when we were tiny, and we swam almost every day.

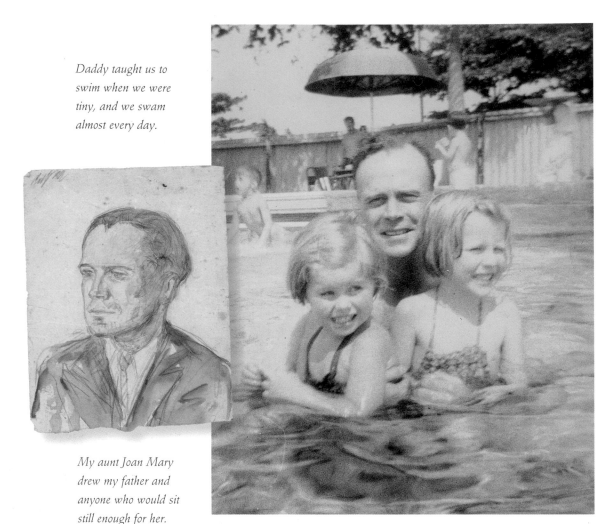

My aunt Joan Mary drew my father and anyone who would sit still enough for her.

The Army School was good and we flourished. When I was six, I was cast in my first role as an actress. I played the Queen in an A.A. Milne poem: 'The King asked the Queen and the Queen asked the Dairymaid: "Could we have some butter for the Royal slice of bread?"'. Mummy made me a beautiful blue satin dress on her Singer sewing machine, and a golden cardboard crown. I was very nervous; but it was that moment, of being in the middle of a story with people listening and watching, that must have smuggled the thought into my mind that from then on I would be an actress.

The King died when we were in Malaya, and it was my father's job to organise the great parade in honour of the Coronation of Queen Elizabeth The Second. Oh! What medals and pencil-sharpeners we had! What mugs and handkerchiefs! It was exciting beyond belief as we had no real idea what London was like, or even where it was. We had the sketchiest concept of royalty, and no notion of smog or snow or good old British fish and chips. I was given a lead model of the golden Coronation State Coach, a thing it seemed to me of

The garden in HQ Malaya was shaping up; we had a gardener called a caboon, who scythed the grass and chewed betel nut with equal energy.

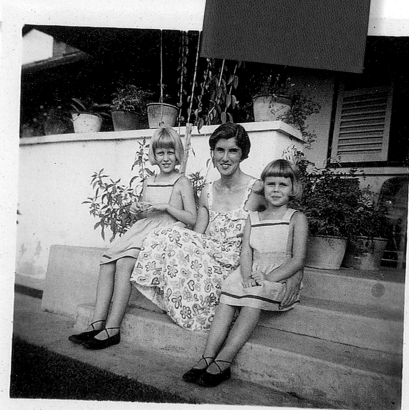

Before we went to dancing classes we had to take salt tablets. My mother was learning to drive and felt that any speed over thirty miles an hour was recklessly dangerous, so journeys were quite sedate. I heard Offenbach's 'Barcarolle' for the first time in the big bungalow where we learned to point our toes and dance the waltz; that music always reminds me of hot dark afternoons, with a storm brewing and lizards on the walls.

unsurpassable beauty. I kept it for years. I may still have it. There was a Fancy Dress party for the children and we went as Norwegian girls (the Voyage of the Kon-Tiki was the book everyone was reading) in outfits made by Mummy on her trusty sewing machine. Our school dresses were made by her as well; and much later in life she was still making things, bed-jackets and jerseys, for friends and family and charity raffles. When it was time for us to go 'home' to England in 1954, the year after the Coronation, when our hair had grown down to our waists but was always worn in plaits, it was a sudden lurch into the unknown again; not exactly scaring, but bringing with it a slash of pain at what you must leave behind, friends, animals and my own beloved country, Malaya. We turned our faces to the west and set sail for Southampton for the last time, on the *Dilwara*, lying at anchor in Singapore's bustling harbour.

Norwegian girl, Queen in blue satin, wood-nymph, dancing girls and princesses with babies. Dressing up was a passion I have not lost to this day. Acting is just pretending to be someone else. We are all actors at some stage of our lives.

Early Days

Outside my aunt's farmhouse, my sister and I wear tunics for my first term at St Mary's. She has a girdle round her waist awarded for Deportment and Courtesy. My hair had just been cut rather savagely and never recovered its earlier childish lustre, not then, not ever.

The thrill of returning to England was vanquished at Southampton: cold and pitilessly grey, thin streaks of skylight spiking the huge arrival hangar, it seemed to me to be a pretty miserable place to call home. But I had reckoned without the staggering charm of late spring, and scented June days, and cuckoo song and roses in hedgerows. My sister and I were sent to board at a small school called Mickledene in the village of Rolvenden in Kent, where my parents eventually bought a house, and where my family lived until the turn of the century.

Mickledene was contained in a small farmhouse and a pair of oast-houses, for drying hops; their roundels had been converted to circular classrooms, and morning assembly was held in what had been a long low barn. Only a few children boarded, and there were three little dormitories called Early Lights, Middle Lights and Late

Boarders' House, Mickledene.

Some postcards demonstrating the bonuses of Mickledene School. The heavy scent of summer roses and the scrubby grass take me back to playing after classes were over before the boarders went in for tea. The bedrooms were cold but I soon got used to them. In the middle bed I dreamed I had a pony of my own. The classrooms stored and exuded the terrifying smell of cabbage, known and dreaded in schools across the nation.

A Bedroom, Mickledene.

Kindergarten, Mickledene.

School House from Playing field, Mickledene

My writing aged nine; my parents were saddened by this style of hand-writing. Later I changed to a more italicised way of writing. The 'X marks the spot' can be checked in the first postcard shown on the page before this.

Sports day at Mickledene. Jacky Binns kneeling holds a tiny silver cup. I am wearing black gym shoes on the left. Mary Steele is standing to Jacky's right. She came on to St Mary's too, where she continued to look rather marvellous in whatever she had to wear.

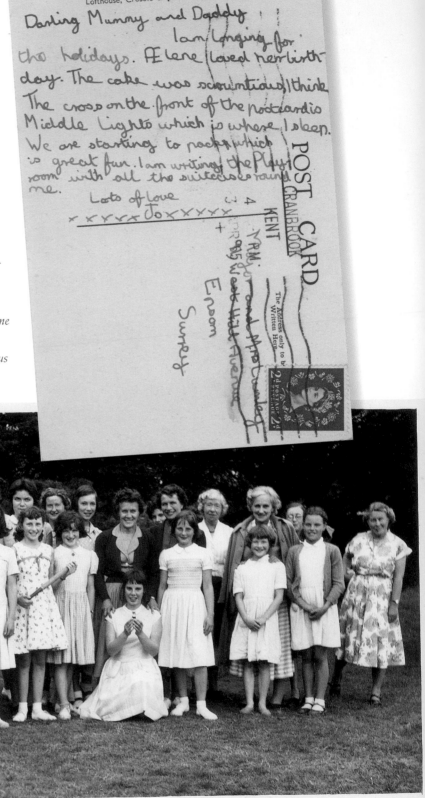

Lights. Lordy! It was cold in those narrow iron beds. Homesickness was a new and unfamiliar demon, and seemed worse when you were longing not just to escape from school but to wish yourself back in a country half a world away, hot steamy Malaya with its monsoons and moonflowers and the clicketty-clack of the Chinese playing Mah-Jong. We learned Shakespeare and French, horrible Maths and lovely Art. We made Mothering Sunday cards and calendars and wrote essays about imaginary islands and wild horses. We were taught to write in rather loopy cursive hand, very inferior to italics, which give you a better template from which you might write clearly, quickly and attractively.

My father had a brief stint in the War Office and we were posted to Epsom; every Sunday we wrote from school to our parents, and walked the mile to church in the village; sometimes we listened to songs on the gramophone, 'The Ugly Duckling' and the 'Isle of Capri', 'Love and Marriage' and 'Che Sera, Sera'. At the end of term we bundled into cars or trains and sped off, to holidays with uncles and aunts, sometimes at Epsom where my mother yearned for the mountains, sometimes in Kent at Court Lodge Farm, where my aunt Joan Mary and her husband Ivor Jehu had bought a farm when they left India. We never had holidays as such, we simply went home from school and that was the holidays. If you did things, it was going to point-to-points or the seaside at Jury's Gap, or a bike ride in the lanes or just mucking about. We never had school holiday projects, and they seem to this day to be

Maybe, on the right, is our only girl cousin. In the holidays we mucked about most of the time, including trespassing into Dougie's Barn where we lit paraffin lamps to give us light amongst the straw bales. I truly believe in guardian angels.

With Mary 'Bony' Hammond, outside the sixth form common room, Pilgrim's Progress. All our rooms were named after holy places, like Bethesda and Carmel, or after letters in the Greek alphabet: Kappa, Lamda, Sigma, Alpha and Epsilon. Bony and I did 'A' level German together, and we were prefects and in the first lacrosse team.

Below: a lacklustre report. My sympathy for the teaching profession knows no bounds.

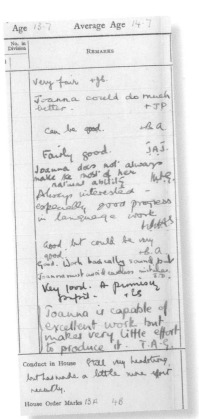

the essence of awfulness, having to think of school every day of the holidays, having to write some ghastly diary or essay, or do sums, or read about the Industrial Revolution when you should be lazing about or dreaming or doing non-school things.

I left Mickledene when I was eleven to go to St Mary's, a convent on the ridge behind Hastings, run by a teaching order of Anglo-Catholic nuns called the Community of the Holy Family. Perhaps because I was three years older, or had got used to the life of a boarder, maybe because the building was so huge in comparison with Mickledene, I felt at home at once and loved my six years there.

There were two hundred girls in the school and of those about seventy boarded. My parents had had to go back to Malaya so Aelene and I spent holidays with friends and relations, and our weekly letters home were now addressed to Depot the Brigade of Gurkhas, Sungei Patani, Malaya. Letters from them to us would be collected from our pigeon-holes after breakfast on Monday mornings, read hastily and stuffed into the blazer pocket with leaking pens, string and sometimes a live mouse. (My mouse was called Reepicheep and a daygirl got her for me: I kept her with my socks and pants in the chest of drawers in the dormitory, which began to smell quite like a dungeon despite the wide-open windows and the gales blowing in past the rhododendrons and pine trees.)

Food was fairly spartan; twenty eggs cracked onto a tray and left for an hour in the oven so that they had to be torn and skewered from the blackened metal was Sunday breakfast after Early Service. We went to chapel often but it became quite normal for us in no time, summoned by bells, running from class to chapel and back, changing for games, clearing away the plates and doing the washing up in the huge echoing pantries with two tea towels to dry up seventy plates and tin forks. We used to go to chapel three times a day, sometimes more. We wore chapel veils, like large handkerchiefs tied over our hair with ribbons, which we were supposed to keep neatly folded so that they could be accessed at a moment's notice, probably for emergency praying. My friend Anthea somehow contrived to semi-destroy every item of clothing as soon as it was put in her ownership, so her crumpled veil was often covered with blotches of ink or grey smudges from pencil sharpenings. Other friends, like Mary Steele and Patricia Summerfield, looked good in whatever they wore, and seemed to grow into the right womanly shape without too much trouble. I was tall, with frizzy hair, spots, unfashionably broad shoulders and was a bit of a lout in retrospect. I don't remember us grieving very much about the way we looked, however: food was poor and so was our skin, but we laughed all the time and slept like the dead and dreamed of becoming gorgeous later.

Ten prefects and the head girl. Left to right, from the back row: Susan Young, Mary Hammond, Kate Crosthwaite, Elizabeth 'Dizzy' Duncan, Sally Hayes, me: in the front, Cordelia Cargill, Pippa Swain, Rosemary Andrew, Gillian McMurray and Jane Strickland. My prefect's badge had been temporarily removed for cigarette-related offences. I wonder if I have spelt all their once-unforgettable names correctly.

The school steps to the terrace, with us looking as lovely as we could. Sugar-stiffened petticoats under summer dresses: the bell about to ring for prep. Not a care in the world.

Being a junior girl in 4B was the best fun in the world: you had no responsibilities, the whole term ahead before your parents would read your school report, a fine array of older girls and prefects to cheek and outwit, a mass of school work which was easy-peasy, woods and pathways winding through bamboo and chestnut trees, rhododendrons and wild garlic on the way to the games field, wood pigeons cooing and floorboards squeaking with the drumming feet of girls in Clarks shoes thumping off to their next assignment. There were too many of us, though: the Babyboomers had arrived, children born the year after the Second World War had ground to its terrible conclusion. The intake into the lowest class when I arrived was forty, not twenty as usual: so we were split up into parallel classes for a year. After that a dreadful thing happened: some of us were skimmed off the top of the form and pushed up a year. I was one of the 'lucky ones' and I never recovered. Because I had always relied on my photographic memory and animal cunning I had always found school work simple (except maths, which trips me up to this day. I can't dial a number without saying it out loud, but am preternaturally gifted at getting roughly the right answer while top bankers flounder). Suddenly we were expected to have absorbed a year's learning in a term and I am afraid I stopped in my tracks and failed from then on. From having come top in most subjects I was now nowhere and I stopped caring too. My bad behaviour attracted many order marks and punishments, some of which were learning poems. Excellent: I could do that in a trice. There was always the school play and the choir, Games, Art and English, French, Latin and German and Italian (lovely languages! I love a language) and fascinating Biology and brow-crumpling Chemistry, History a mystery as I read books like *The Robe* and *Gone With the Wind* under the desk, and Geography with maps of islands to be outlined in Caran D'Ache Azure Blue.

A wide hairband was a fruitless way of trying to tame my very bad hair. Expression hoping to emulate Claudia Cardinale, as I knew Brigitte Bardot was well beyond reach at this stage.

Second right: I try to look like Aaron in the school play. Adetoun Fagbayi and Aronke Alade hold peacock fans, and Imogen Newbatt, heavily bearded and our version of Judi Dench, played Moses in Christopher Fry's Firstborn. I went on playing men, and got used to wearing moustaches. Much later in life, Patsy emerged as having been a man for a spell in her chequered past.

The Sisters of the Holy Community were exceptional women. They had the pastoral care of a large number of girls and yet they had never been parents themselves. They took no hostages and what they said, went: but I don't remember any nun being unkind or unfair. On the contrary, they were miraculously even-tempered and good humoured, full of enthusiasm and encouragement; their minds were always on their own calling, the selfless service of their Saviour, and their vows were threefold then, as they are now: poverty, chastity and obedience, symbolized by the three knots worn in the girdle round their waists. They owned nothing. Their blue bedspreads would become their coffin covering, their food was what we wouldn't eat (not much, despite much of it being really grim) and their comforts were few. Sister Elizabeth sometimes kept sweets in her long pocket which swung under her grey floor-length habit, and in the summer when they thought no-one was looking they would roll up their skirts and play cricket. Terms passed, and juniors became seniors and I was eventually made a prefect ('Set a thief to catch a thief' said Sister Jesse succinctly). Inexorably responsibilities mounted up, lists had to be made and registers taken, rules were to be enforced and miscreants to be punished, and suddenly the poacher had become game-keeper.

Looking back it strikes me how often in our lives we start again from scratch. At no stage of my grown-up life have I wielded the power we

Fiddling about with my Slazenger racquet in a tennis match. Is that Caroline Moule as my partner? Amazingly I got colours for netball, lacrosse and tennis despite being uncompetitive and fairly lazy due to trying to look cool in front of junior girls. It was considered rather a poor show to be seen to be trying too hard at games.

Summer dress and blazer outside Pilgrim's Progress. Hair now trapped in a beehive of sorts. I must have been sixteen. The school gardens were huge and shady and sunny and full of secret corners.

45

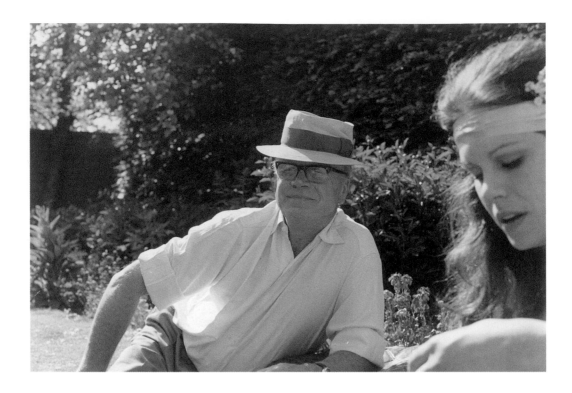

On the lawn at Sparkeswood, the house my parents bought when my father left the Army. Signs of flower power are showing in my headband with blossoms tucked in. My father would wear any old hat he found in the hall. He loved gardening, but got to the stage where he couldn't bear to kill any living thing, even daisies and buttercups, by cutting the grass.

had as prefects, swishing about in our pleated skirts and twinsets like middle-aged women, demanding respect and subservience. You start school as a baby aged five and leave aged seventeen going on sixty. Then you start again in the wide, wide world as a green and innocent beginner, behaving like a child, with new boyfriends and hair in bunches and immature thoughts about how the world should be run ('Let's share everything! Let's stay up all night and not pay taxes! Let's go round the world like gypsies and never settle down in boring jobs!') and slowly the world turns and suddenly you are struggling with forms to fill in and bills to pay. Your own children grow, and eat like wolves; and life seems like hard work with none of the rewards you thought would come your way simply by being a grown-up. Then comes the time to retire, and back you go again, holding hands on the beach and laughing as you eat apples with your dentures firmly attached by glue to your gums; sometimes television shows geared for the very young are more appealing than the alien humour and scary news programmes that make up the menu in the listings. Then, as Shakespeare noted, we are back to being big babies again, balding and in need of care and changing and feeding, and one day, so soon that you may be able to see the beginning of your life at the same time, the end comes, and That's All There Was. There has to be a way of looking at it to make a story, to make sense of it.

How we longed to be like the film stars of those days! We dipped our nylon petticoats in sugar-water and dried them on radiators to make them stiff so our skirts would stick out like Brigitte Bardot's pink gingham dress. Bardot! But her baby-ish pout and bed-time hair said Young Creature, not svelte siren of forty. Even then, women were beginning to try to look young, rather than mature. True, Sophie Loren looked utterly *femme fatale* but she was not our icon, nor was Marilyn Monroe with her curves and thick lipstick. It was Bardot then and still is now, fifty years later. And just as my school days were drawing to a close, the Beatles arrived with Love Me Do (Oh! How thrilling! I do love you, mop-top charmers from Liverpool even though I have never really been anywhere in Britain except school and the south. I love you, and I love the thought of London, waiting huge and wicked like a distant stalker with sweets). The pantheon of Buddy Holly and the Everly Brothers, Little Richard, Cliff and even Elvis had to be reshuffled so that the new world order of pop music could accommodate the irresistible and magnetic cheeky-boys. Shimmering behind them, almost coming into focus, was the New World, of flower power and mini-skirts, and streets paved with promises. I would fit in there: somehow I would fit in there nicely.

When I left school I joined the family in Italy on the first holiday we had ever had. Schooldays faded away like footprints in the sand and the idea of what to do to earn money had not yet crossed my mind. I was inching nearer to my dream of being mistaken for a French woman whilst wearing sunglasses and nail varnish, the acme of sophistication. Still reading: always reading (and what looks like drinking too).

Make-up & Mini-skirts

*Boots: 'model's own',
but we didn't say that
in those days. These
yellow boots from Biba
were my favourites and
look a bit shabby in the
picture through constant
wear. It was expensive
to buy shoes just for
photographs: no models
were rich enough to do
that. Today you would
never be expected to
accessorise your own
shots.*

The flat we moved into in 1964 was just off the Earl's Court Road. It
was on the fourth floor with no lift, and four of us shared it: Nina,
Dinx, Aelene and me, squashed into two bedrooms, with a rented gas
stove and no fridge. Paradise! I have never felt quite the same thrill
as waking at dawn to scurry off to my first ever modelling job at
the department store Debenham and Freebody, hearing the muffled
announcements of the Underground station which roared away far
below, seeing the scruffy rooftops and dusty pigeons and slapping on
make-up by candlelight so that I wouldn't wake the others sleeping.
After a month of training at Lucie Clayton I had been taken on as a
model, just as skirts were creeping up above the knee and no-one, my
dear, but no-one wanted to be seen without false eyelashes. (Actually,
only models wore them at the time: but it is very easy, in your
enthusiasm and excitement, to believe that the WHOLE WORLD cares
about your new shade of eye-shadow, and will be watching every step
of your mock-Courreges boots as you patter past shops called Carrot
on Wheels and Granny Takes a Trip, hair in rollers under a headscarf, a
man's watch weighing down your skinny wrist, pale-lipsticked mouth
shouting 'Taxi!!!' as you race from job to job.)

London was on fire with excitement. A new Labour Government had
been elected, the Keeler affair was recent history, the music and fashion
and drop-dead fabness of the city was matched nowhere on earth, or so
it seemed to us. True, as models we weren't paid a king's ransom but it
was a great deal more than most people earned. It was considered very
vulgar to talk about money in those days, so if you had it you picked up
the tab and kept quiet. If you didn't, and were as skint as boracic lint, you
dressed extravagantly in home-altered clothes, and made your own self
into a work of art, or at least individuality, with necklaces and headbands,
frills, hats, sunglasses and serious posing. Looking back at these pictures,

87

JOANNA
LUMLEY

Height	5' 8"	Hauteur	173
Bust	34"	Poitrine	86
Waist	24"	Taille	61
Hips	35"	Hanches	89
Shoes	5	Chaussures	38
Gloves	7	Gants	7
Hair	Dark Blonde	Cheveux	Blonds Foncés
Eyes	Blue-Grey	Yeux	Bleu-Gris

HEADSHOT BY VIC SINGH-FULL LENGTH SHOT BY CLIVE ARROWSMITH

LUCIE CLAYTON   01-629 0667/8

*We had model cards giving
our statistics, with flattering
photographs to show how
good we could look. My
size 5 feet were sometimes
crammed into smaller
shoes: the ones worn with
thick white socks were
actually size three. But it
was for* Queen *magazine,
photographed by Clive
Arrowsmith, so who was
complaining.*

I wonder: how did I manage to pull it off? I didn't even have a hair-dryer. In the flat, we shared our clothes, tights and shoes and bags… we put one pound each into the kitty every week and scraped by on bread and cheese, as happy as skylarks, walking if we couldn't afford the bus or tube. Three years later, I had my own Mini (given in lieu

Below: in the kitchen at Earl's Court, with Nina and her then boyfriend, now husband, Hamish. We aimed to look like doped existentialists: the walls and floor were gloss yellow and I was clearly longing to look like an actress suffering from strangeness. Serious posing. Taken by my boyfriend Michael.

Sometimes (left) I posed with statues and furniture. Look at the length of the skirt. In Paris I was nearly arrested for my abbreviated hemline.

of a debt owed by a photographer friend; value £120, and too groovy to be true to have your own MINI, like top model Jean 'The Shrimp' Shrimpton), and I had my own Carmen rollers and hairpieces, as we all had to do our own hair and make-up; and my passport was franked with stamps from every country in Europe, and you would say 'D'accord' instead of 'yeah', and be sent on trips to Portugal or Austria at a day's notice. But it was all a bit home-made, and people were not as terrified as people are today of getting it wrong or looking ridiculous. And there was just less money, less emphasis on criticising the way people looked, less bitchery and sour grapes. Women's magazines contained

These three pictures were taken by Crispian Woodgate, a friendly Daily Mail *photographer, who kindly took some test shots of me in the countryside. His Mini later became mine when he couldn't repay money I had lent him. Even snappers had it rough sometimes.*

If any photos were acceptable they would be enlarged and put into the heavy modelling book each girl lugged about with her. The cotton dress belonged to my flatmate Dinx, a dancer with the London Festival Ballet. It was cold, I remember, but you never complained.

romantic stories, recipes, knitting patterns, an agony aunt, and fashion in the shape of crimpelene dresses and polyester cardigans. We were, as models, expected to bring along our own junk jewellery and boots, scarves, gloves, tights and belts, and as we tended to wear these things in real life, as it were, the photographs lacked a certain presentational gloss (unless you were working for *Queen* or *Vogue*, or *Elle*, for heaven's sake, when you would be overseen and styled by sharp leaders of fashion; and the unease and fear that skittered through those photoshoots was more The Devil Wears Prada than Colour Co-Ordinates in Bri-Nylon).

The looks we did: baby doll, gawky schoolgirl, bride-to-be, young mum, sophisticated hostess, person laughing at fruit, girls having fun, sporty, silly student, happy families — with Dad in a home-knitted slipover and huge children in crochet — glamorous business woman, smart secretary, funky half-wit, zonked-out druggy, freckled thing. Egged on by the photographers (the snappers), we flung our legs and arms about, peered round pillars, gasped at vegetables, smirked on gangways and lolled on paper backdrops. It was the best job you could have, if you wanted your brain to have a holiday…but slow down: I have drifted into a sort of patronising rant about a job which was hard work and exacting, demanding professionalism every minute of every day, which was creative and artistic, sometimes frightening but mostly very good fun.

I had the good fortune to become, for a short while, the house model for Jean Muir, one of the great fashion icons of the twentieth century, renowned for her silk jersey dresses and effortless chic. She made the garments using me as a clothes horse, pinning and adjusting, snipping and shaping the fabric while I stood stock still; and then it was my task to help pack the dresses for delivery, and model them in the tiny showroom for fashion editors from the grandest magazines and shops. She had a profound impact on me, with her insistence on excellence and beauty, proportion and detail. Nothing escaped her eagle eye and many people found her rather terrifying, including me. But underneath her steely exterior beat a heart full of compassion and kindness, impervious to trendiness and negativity. She had a devout circle of clients, nick-named The Muirettes, from every walk of life,

Shoes: model's own. I adored these Biba shoes. They made me 6ft 2 inches and I undid the hems of trousers so that they dropped over the shoe to the ground: it looked as if I were walking on stilts. The dress I have to this day, Jean Muir at her most gloriously fluid and colourful, silk, with a large square silk scarf I have tied around my head like factory worker in WW2.

I love this picture of me and Miss Muir; she always dressed in navy blue in London, and her ruler-straight hairstyle never changed. Her eyebrows were pencil thin and her lipstick was always dark reddish–brown.

and like many other important artists I have met she had a wide interest in world politics, literature, philosophy, music, theatre, cooking and fun. Jean was my friend from the moment I met her until her death. After she had left the stage, there was talk of continuing the label Jean Muir without her, and indeed for a year or so clothes came out bearing her name and a likeness to her designs. But without her, we all knew that nothing could replace her, and after one glorious last party the tents were packed up and the caravan moved on. Some things are of their own time for a reason. An archive collection of her clothes was given by Harry Leuckert, her husband, to the Museum of Scotland in Edinburgh. At the opening ceremony of the exhibition it was strange to walk amongst museum exhibits which had been part of my young life, as if I too had become part of the show.

If I ate as much as everyone else, I think I would be a heavyweight sumo wrestler. Like all models, and most actresses, I am aware that being a bit fatter than you should be is multiplied hugely by the cruel lens of the camera. The camera puts on half a stone at least. To combat this unwanted porkiness, we used all sorts of tricks to keep

"Every woman should have a Jean Muir in her wardrobe"
Joanna Lumley

Jean Muir
A Fashion Icon

7 November 2008–15 March 2009
Chambers Street Edinburgh
www.nms.ac.uk/jeanmuir

Part of the catalogue which accompanied the exhibition of Jean's archive in Edinburgh. The photographs were taken in her London flat, scrupulously bare and white with touches of patterned lace and mirrored furniture. She liked the make-up ballet dancers wear. Almost all of her clothes were shown with navy or black tights.

Why can't I remember who made this painting of me? I do recall dressing up as a sort of Lady of Shalott figure, with brow-band and a rose. Many of the pop songs of that era mentioned knights in white satin, ravens and jesters, and sad-eyed ladies of the lowlands. He made my upper lip too long, I think. I don't have the painting: I wonder who does.

Overleaf: the friendly world of fashion – sensible clothes for nice women with a penchant for artificial fabrics.

thin: my time was before the eating of tissues (that must have been very grim) but I ate Limmit slimming biscuits for lunch, and hardly drank at all. Diets rampaged: the grapefruit diet, the steak diet, the slimming injections, the amphetamine pills, the empty stomach when your tummy would gurgle and groan during a shoot....but in all my time as a model I only knew one anorexic girl. To be thin was good, but not THAT important. No-one I knew suffered from bulimia, and yet the snappers would tease us about our immense fatness when we measured only 35 inches round the hips. Thick panstik make-up covered loitering spots, and before photo-shopping was an everyday practice the studios laboured diligently to re-touch by hand the black-and-white prints to be passed on, perfect, to the client. No wonder girls with pearly skin and shiny hair were at the top of the profession: but even those of us thuggishly attired in wigs and painted freckles found work, three jobs a day, £5 an hour, bring your own black polo-neck and don't be late. We were only ever paid six months later, for some unfathomable reason, so we were always anxious to get work to fill the gaping coffers which hard-eyed bank managers refused to understand: perpetually robbing Peter to pay Paul. Whenever there was any money to spare we spent it. Who wanted to pay taxes anyway? No point in saving it! We would be rich enough for ever!

Or so we thought.

Catching the mood

a long
hot
sum

Focus on new Britain. Focus on young designers. Focus on the 21 Shops. Now strategically placed all over Britain. At WOOLLANDS, Knightsbridge. At Marshall & Snelgrove, Oxford Street W1, New Street, Birmingham, and now St. Anne's Place, Manchester, also Williams & Hopkins, Bournemouth. Dynamic young fashion ideas. Quick! Look what's in *now*. Wow!

Well, it just had to come... the little plastic dress

The craze for PVC has reached its zenith. We've had plastic macs, boots, bags and hats, now comes the plastic dress.

This joky little dress is great for the girl who moves around at such a rate she doesn't have time for ironing. It's great for any mother with sticky-fingered children.

When it gets dirty you just wipe it down.

Available at...

PICTURE BY CRISPIAN WOODGATE

DAILY

nday
onoré

matt surface.
So caramel, navy, brown or black, sizes 8-16. About 17 gns from your favourite fashion shop. Torridon, St. Honoré, which
this space tomorrow.

PAGE 8

FEMAIL *fashion*

These
shoes

How w

Here the 'Top Twelve' by greatest
Harelle
fashio
store
Ask
the
an

Left: The little boy style is a smash... for next season. In a pinky wool jersey worn with a grey silk and around with a belt below. A simply shaped dress knitted in a pretty stripe. With black and grey details... with the design right. Shades of the Thirties, in nuts for the 'new' season, in soft quilts in slip style tunic blouse. Other styles in silk nylon. Black and in the...
Other colours include... blush/grey £2.3.6. *continued*

DAILY MAIL

WHAT IS A MODEL?

Second in Veronica Scott's series on the new models: Joanna Lumley

Extravagant prints, off-beat colours—*these are Jo Lumley's formulae for dressing-up clothes (which, after all, aren't intended to be overlooked!) Persian print Banlon trouser suit, Hildebrand, 10-14, 10½ gn.*

Likes unusual styles based on peasant themes that people notice. *Born under Taurus, Jo's extrovert, articulate —and her clothes are vivid too. Mexican smock and headscarf, printed cotton, comes from Granny Takes a Trip at World's End, Chelsea, 6½ gn. Openwork, natural colour, straw picture hat, Eaton Bag Co., 1 gn.*

22

JO LUMLEY, born in India twenty years ago, signed on with the Lucie Clayton model agency, began her modelling career in London by store modelling: 9-5.30, £8 a week.

First break came a few months later when a photographer asked her to pose for the cover of a book. It was never published, but it was her debut just the same. Today she's a regular WOMAN favourite.

With the same photographer she went to Moscow to photograph five fur coats in six days—a leisurely routine compared with her hectic photographic trips for catalogues.

Jo is a natural mimic and story-teller, recounting films, books and playing all parts like a full dramatic cast. She wants to be a film director. Vital, vulnerable, she is subject to thumping great fits of depression, dissecting and denigrating herself from head to toe—fat head, spotty face, prizefight shoulders, deformed ribcage, huge hips, bottle legs, tiny flipper feet—that's Jo, according to Jo. Actually, she is beautiful— warm, lively and womanly-looking. But she longs to be thin and can't stay that way. No wonder! She has a colossal schoolgirl appetite, con-sumes cheese by the pound (having given up sticky paste which she declares she "lived on" at school!).

Jo's "hung up" on ghosts and gob-lins, reads hands with sensational confidence and frequently calls everyone "Baby Doll" in fast-talking American.

Yet despite her exuberant nuttiness, Jo is full of the ingredients of the corny but very real "girl next door" who's always resolving a new fashion plan and always ending up with some-thing else! Jo knows all the fashion rules, but she's Jo, and she dresses that way. Her fashion urges are original, chaotically colourful like she is—*and to my mind they prove that simple restrained elegance is not the be-all of the fashion story.*

There's a gaping place for *personal* experiment with colour, for impudent adventure in trying out unusual

The fashion for making dresses out of Indian bedspreads was at its height. This one came from Granny Takes a Trip. Heavy green-blue eyes lined with kohl, lime-green shift, scarlet PVC coat and rather saggy-fronted denim skirt with a jaunty John Lennon cap…that was what it was to be a model in 1965.

Woman — July 22 1967

Likes fine jersey shifts for day, *sleeveless or long sleeves. Must be very short, zip down back for quick dressing. Jersey dress, Simon Jeffrey, 10-14, 94s. 6d. Felt Cordoba, Edward Mann,* 35s. 11d. **Feels undressed without straps across her shoes.** *Shoes, Saxone, 2½-8½, 59s. 11d.*

styles; there's even room for mistakes if it's not the end of the piggybank.

Jo, stomping up the ruined, rocky Phoenician city of Solunto in Sicily in thick leather brogues plus huge lizard portmanteau handbag to pose in those "Persian" pantaloons at top of the page; Jo, swinging through the jam-packed streets of Palermo in Mexican smock and hat, left, to pose and show you her relaxwear, is a genuine original. Her fashion says so.

It may not be your style. But then, again, it may.

Next week: Newcomer Jenny Fussell

Prefers scruffy old clothes for weekends, *but picked this shadow-striped denim skirt with buttoned hip pockets, crepon shirt, PVC raincoat as having the suitable "knockabout" air. Skirt, Dorothy Perkins, 22-28 in. waist, 29s. 11d.; shirt, by Lewis Separates, 34-38 in. bust, 14s. 11d.; coat, Dannimac, 10-14, 79s. 6d. Scarf, Aldbrook.*

23

She doesn't know...

...she does know **PATONS** –the greatest name in hand knits

that's why she knitted her sweater* in Patons Totem Double Crepe. But she doesn't know that Patons spin not only wool and cashmere but nearly all the newest fibres for nearly all the biggest names in knitwear.

*Published by Patons in 'Fashion Knits' No. 12

PATONS –the name you don't see on the label

MORLEY
A clever co-ordination of stripes in varying widths makes a new twinset concept in 'Bri-Nylon'. Colours: orange fizz, parma, navy, spice. Sizes: 36-40 inches. Style Nos.: Sweater B 932, Cardigan B 933. Approximate retail prices: Sweater £2.9.6. Cardigan £2.19.6.

COLOUR CO-ORDINATES IN **BRI** NYLON*

Facing page and inset: Pure white in 'Bri-Nylon' is crisply striped with self pattern and has matching ribbed knee socks. Colours: powder blue, white, carnation, green, daffodil, navy or coffee. Sizes: Sweater 36-40 inches. Stockings in medium and large. Style reference: Dandy. Approximate retail prices: Sweater £2.2.6, Stockings 5s 11d.

The roller-skating pictures were taken by one of the giants of the decade, David Montgomery. Tinka Patterson smiles past the diamonds at my ear; I grasp freezing steering wheels in a scrap yard (and later I was to be in Steptoe and Son *for real): and I do my best in nylon and wool. Thrilling.*

Only one of these girls will be able to . . .

Breakaway GIRLS HATE SNOBS—LOVE STEPTOE AND SON

To stun them in: ask any Breakaway girl what's cool in fibre kicks and she'll tell you Bri-Nylon chiffon. This gorgeously dotty dress weighs less than a bit of fluff—it's calculated to lift any girl out of the dumps. It's designed for evening shifts, but everyone would be thrilled to see her in it earlier.

'Who says I'm down in the dumps?'

Don't say a thing:

When thoughts are too deep for words, jewellery from Bensons speaks for you. It makes the great unmistakable gesture.
It's for keeps.
Bensons have been helping to express strong silent emotions in hard enduring stones for 126 years.
People know it's the place to go when only the finest necklaces, rings, brooches, bracelets and watches will do. The necklace and the ring saying so much in the picture are diamonds set in platinum. Bensons, at 25 Old Bond Street, W.1, are full of eloquent things.

just
give her
diamonds
from **Bensons**

...stand still!

It's awful hard to stand still in Actionwear. Specially when the Actionwear has been tailored into slacks by Slimma. It's awful hard not to skate, slide, twist, twirl, wheel, whirl, flurry, hurry . . . when you're wearing slacks like these. Because Actionwear _loves_ to move. And the Actionwear fabric springs back after anything. Yes, _anything._

Actionwear
NYLON
CHEMSTRAND

Slimma Other colours: black, navy, red, pale blue, chocolate and dark green. Size 10 to 16. Price is 55/-

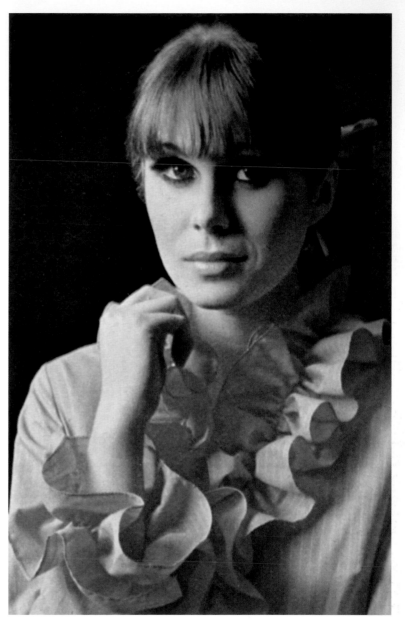

*For the Daily Mail 'Rag Doll' series with a red rinse in the hair: in
Duffy's shoot styled by Molly Parkin for the photographic spread Bailey
said was the best of the year. Paulene Stone scrubs her teeth and I comb
my red wig. These were daring and ground-breaking pictures at the time.
And here I am again in frills and a wonky fringe.*

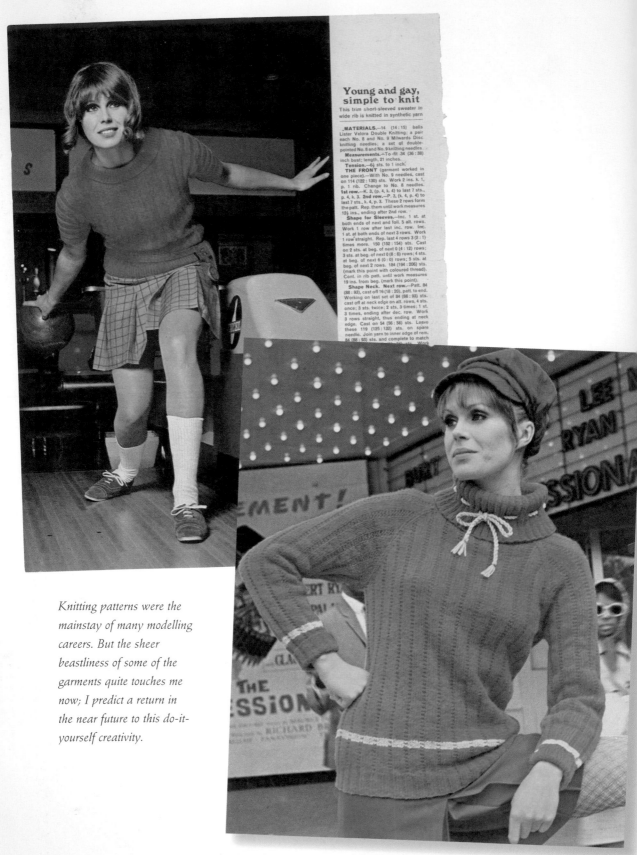

Young and gay, simple to knit

This trim short-sleeved sweater in wide rib is knitted in synthetic yarn

MATERIALS.—14 (14:15) balls Lister Velora Double Knitting; a pair each No. 8 and No. 9 Milwards Disc knitting needles; a set of double-pointed No. 8 and No. 9 knitting needles.

Measurements.—To fit 34 (36:38) inch bust; length, 21 inches.

Tension.—6½ sts. to 1 inch.

THE FRONT (garment worked in one piece).—With No. 9 needles, cast on 114 (122:130) sts. Work 2 ins. k. 1, p. 1 rib. Change to No. 8 needles.

1st row.—K. 3, (p. 4, k. 4) to last 7 sts., p. 4, k. 3. **2nd row.**—P. 3, (k. 4, p. 4) to last 7 sts., k 4, p. 3. These 2 rows form the patt. Rep. them until work measures 12½ ins., ending after 2nd row.

Shape for Sleeves.—Inc. 1 st. at both ends of next and foll. 5 alt. rows. Work 1 row after last inc. row. Inc. 1 st. at both ends of next 3 rows. Work 1 row straight. Rep. last 4 rows 3 (2 : 1) times more. 150 (152:154) sts. Cast on 2 sts. at beg. of next 0 (4 : 12) rows; cast 3 sts. at beg. of next 0 (8 : 6) rows; 4 sts. at beg. of next 6 (0 : 0) rows; 5 sts. at beg. of next 2 rows. 184 (194 :206) sts. (mark this point with coloured thread). Cont. in rib patt. until work measures 19 ins. from beg. (mark this point).

Shape Neck. Next row.—Patt. 84 (88 : 93), cast off 16 (18 : 20), patt. to end. Working on last set of 84 (88 : 93) sts. cast off at neck edge on alt. rows, 4 sts. once; 3 sts. twice; 2 sts. 3 times; 1 st. 3 times, ending after dec. row. Work 3 rows straight, thus ending at neck edge. Cast on 54 (56 : 58) sts. Leave these 119 (125 :132) sts. on spare needle. Join yarn to inner edge of rem. 84 (88 : 93) sts. and complete to match. Work

Knitting patterns were the mainstay of many modelling careers. But the sheer beastliness of some of the garments quite touches me now; I predict a return in the near future to this do-it-yourself creativity.

A much later and more glamorous shoot on Mauritius with Patrick Lichfield. I worked with him more than almost any other photographer: he was amazingly good company, very funny, and charming to all he met. Here Jane Raphaely, fashion editor for South Africa's Fair Lady *magazine, steadies a glass of wine as we watch the* Sega *being danced by firelight on the beach. In the same shoot I sit with fruit and flowers, and listen to a sea-shell. I always longed for straight hair, never really achieved it.*

Compare these two photographs: taken at different times and with different models, all except me. Below, Sue Murray, Sandra Paul, later Mrs Michael Howard, and Paulene Stone look gorgeous on a Rolls Royce while I, slightly lower-ranking and not as gorgeous, skulk behind on the bonnet. On the left, we look as though we are avatars of the picture on the right, all except Grace Coddington, Amazing Grace, now second in command at American Vogue, *the funky unpredictable short-haired knitter, the only model who could make a ball of yarn look cool. Jane Lumb in the centre in yellow is a dead ringer for Sue Murray in blue on the Rolls headlamp, with her arm bent to hide a rolled-over waistband. We were all almost interchangeable; almost, but utterly not. I was shelves behind any of these more famous faces. Happy as a clam to be in their company.*

Admiration was reserved for those of us who could change our looks as much and as often as possible. Wigs and hairpieces were swapped and borrowed to give us New Looks. I found hair shoots chilling as hairdressers ('crimpers') sometimes misjudged just how much of a handful my hair was. It could stay up in the air if sprayed within an inch of its life, and they had no compunction about cutting bits off that they had failed to curl or set properly. I can truthfully say that my hair, and how it looks, has governed a large part of my professional life, as feeble as that sounds. Bad Hair Life is putting it too strongly: but the menace of the follicles is always with me. My hair will dance on my grave.

3

4

1 Joseph at Salon 33 makes a short centre parting; flicks the hair up at one side, and then divides the other side into near-ringlets

2 Using the same short parting, he catches one side of the hair into a short, fanned-out ponytail, and brushes the other side forward

3 At André Bernard, they're in love with the 1940s look. Stylist Colin uses big 1966 rollers to set a curly, wavy Rita Hayworth style

4 The same set is swooshed round into a curly "up" style. The hair is secured high on the left side, combed out into feathery curls

The kindest way of looking at these is to wonder if she could have made a career in espionage.

Yellow wig, black fright wig, clumps
of hairpieces cunningly flopped onto
the fringe, dyed dark brown, and
frothed into lunatic boiling curls...
I did all these hairstyles to look
different, but underneath: same old
face. Very rare canary legs and a
sort of gossamer shift...those were the
days. Shoes (model's own) still rather
shabby.

Sometimes, however, the pictures took a more interesting turn. These, by Lidbrooke, were for an article about the psychology of sex in clothes. The PVC coat and star-studded sheer shift are a country mile away from cosy jerseys and tweed skirts. Lidbrooke took a morning to set up the shot, then only took seven or eight frames, very unusual in the age when 40 or 50 rolls per shot was commonplace. The photographer couldn't know for sure until the contact sheet came back from the darkroom whether or not the pictures were what he or she wanted. In the starry dress I think I look a bit like a centaur, half horse, half woman.

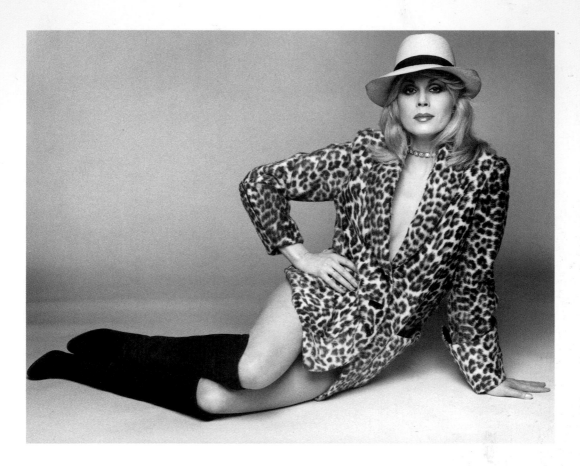

Looking glamorous meant no smiling and quite a lot
of staring deep into the lens. The fake leopard coat
was a favourite garment, worn with my mother's
choker of paste diamonds. When it was stolen I
was very set down. Black knee boots will never go
out of fashion, only the heels and shapes of the toes
change. My poppy-covered blouse had been made to
order; my hair had just been cut short and I think I
felt uneasy about its new length. Crimpers often cut
hair too short because I think they get carried away
by the sharpness of their scissors. My panama hat
was a trade mark and for a short while I was the
only holder of a British passport with the subject
wearing a hat.

I collected old Victorian chemises and shirts: this strange picture shows a lovely Persian wall hanging and a doubtful woman in dodgy lighting.

Opposite, on holiday in Greece, in 1966, aged twenty, as ever practising to be better at my chosen career as somebody, anybody, in front of a camera.

Always present a moving target: don't get stuck with 'a look': keep changing and they won't find you out. I still have the blue and white Liberty Jean Muir dress with puffed sleeves, but the grey straw hat has gone with the wind. Lurex cut low, cowboy gear and lariat, Gypsy Rose Lee…there was nothing we wouldn't wear or do. Modelling stood me in good stead for my future career in the changeable profession of acting.

And Introducing...

'Let's start at the very beginning...' Looking as casual as a first-timer can , smokes on the ground, paint-stained, what-the-heck jeans, Pinewood Studios here I come. Only one line to say: and the door to the profession swings open.

In the old days, if, in your screen debut, you played an important part, it always said in the credits '...and introducing So-and-So as "Lorinda Gazebo"' or whatever the character was called. If the first role you played was not of a noteworthy size this didn't happen. As I had sloped in through the back door, as it were, was in fact blown up before the front credits rolled in my first film 'Some Girls Do', I was denied the peculiar thrill of being introduced to a grateful audience at the beginning of a dazzling career. I hadn't been to drama school, or been in repertory theatre; I had been a photographic model, which in those faraway times was considered the most pitiful and unhelpful background for an aspiring actress to have had. You had to belong to the actors' union, Equity, to work: and you couldn't get your Equity card unless you had spent 42 weeks in the theatre, or had played a speaking part in a film, but you couldn't be cast in a film because you didn't have a card... it was a Catch 22 conundrum. The change of direction from modelling to acting had been playing on my mind for some months. I had been in several television commercials and thought that I could use that brief experience to blag my way into the film world, but the Equity card, or lack of it, was the barrier. Then suddenly a knight in shining armour appeared in the handsome form of the great Shakespearean actor Richard Johnson. I met him at a party in Chelsea and told him how hard I was finding it to get over the threshold into the world of entertainment. He said 'I'm doing a film at the moment: I'll get you to be a small character with a line to say, and then you will be given an Equity card'. And that is exactly what happened. The film, 'Some Girls Do', was a Bulldog Drummond story and my part was a robot who fiddled about with wires and blew the building up at the command of some sinister officer played by James Villiers. My line was 'Yes, Mr Robinson' so perhaps he wasn't an officer, but I had my card! I was a professional actress!

In my black jump-suit for the English Girl in On Her Majesty's Secret
Service. *This Angel of Death wore a jewelled Spanish comb and short black
high-heeled boots. Still attached to a cigarette, more for show than for smoking;
the blur in the background is the Bond lovelies in the huge revolving room at the
top of the Schilthorn peak, called Piz Gloria. Handsome George Lazenby took
over from Sean Connery as Bond: watch the film again and see how well he did.
Telly Savalas as Blofeld was a chilling blend of menacing charm and cruelty;
the film is held by afficionados to be one of the best James Bond films ever made.
The added poignancy of the death of Bond's new bride (played by Diana Rigg)
makes it the only one that ends on a tragic note. And Louis Armstrong sang
'We have all the time in the world…' Fab.*

We often lined up to do publicity shots like these. Sometimes the same picture printed in black and white gave magazines the chance to make it look like a fresh shoot.

The sensational Piz Gloria circled by the mountains of the Bernese Oberland. Even today it boasts of its proud links with James Bond.

With the optimism of youth I imagined it would always be possible to work if you were punctual, talented and polite. To be cast as a Bond girl was a stroke of sheer good luck, as London was crammed with pretty would-be starlets and any one of hundreds of girls could have played an Angel Of Death in Blofeld's glamorous army of assassins trained in germ warfare. There were twelve of us; and in the superb story 'On Her Majesty's Secret Service' we were garrisoned at Blofeld's secret hideaway in the Swiss Alps for two months. Autumn gave way to winter, and the Bernese Oberland changed from golden-orange to grey, black and white. Every day we were up before dawn to put on fairly extravagant costumes and make-up, and have our hair done: then we caught a cable car up to the summit of the Schilthorn, a cage full of twittering birds of paradise, supervised by a character called Irma Bunt, grim thuggish warden of Blofeld's experimental clinic. It was completely thrilling to be involved in such a colossal extravaganza. The village of Murren where we were based was sealed off from the outside world for six months, Bond's Aston Martin was airlifted in, stuntmen arrived by helicopter, the circus had come to town. (Forty years later, when I was travelling on a ferry in Sudan, my arms were grasped by an enthusiastic Arab who recognised me as a Bond girl, even though I had only spoken two or three lines in my part as the English Girl: so great was the impact of those films.)

Blofeld's 'Angels of Death'
The Piz Gloria Girls

Saltzman. She met with him and was offered a five-year contract, from which Saltzman was subsequently forced to release her. The contract didn't exactly [...] a vast amount of work, [...] her brief part in *OHMSS*, [...] go Jenny unbelievably [...] that must be the worst [...] of them all!" Curiously [...] ere as the Italian girl, on [...] credits of *OHMSS* she is [...] girl. Her other films [...] of *Dracula* (1970) with [...] *Percy's Progress* (1974) [...] Madeline Smith, and [...]tles (1974). On TV in [...] ound fame as co-host of [...] *Magpie* and has also [...]rsuaders.

[...] Dinah Sheridan and [...]ley, her brother is [...]irman of

[...]dinavian girl

[...]ay, Jule Ege's [...]oluminous to list here, [...] *Home Should Have One* [...] *World Forgot* (1971), [...] *Deadly Sins* (1971) [...] *Up Pompeii* (1971) [...]mith, *Go For A Take* [...]ska Hempel, *Percy's* [...]enny Hanley and [...] TV appearances [...] in the comedy

[...] (Zara)

[...] determined

[...] (Mona Chong)

[...] includes brief [...]ly (1969) and The [...]69) with Diana [...] Curt Jurgens.

[...]ces where The Piz Gloria girls are named, these are as they **appear in the combined continuity version of the script. Names were probably only inserted to simplify identification, since in the actual film most remain anonymous.**

[...] Hanley was first spotted in a cinema commercial by a talent scout for Harry

6. "Course I know what he's allergic to."
SUE-ANN, the English girl
(Joanna Lumley)

Clearly believing her role in *OHMSS* insignificant - she has described it as "only set dressing, like a vase of bright cushions" - Joanna Lumley has appeared in a handful of feature films. Among them are *Some Girls Do* (1968), *The Breaking of Bumbo* (1970), *Games that Lovers Play* (1972), *The Satanic Rites of Dracula* (1973). However, it is her consistent work in TV that has made her a household name. She has had starring roles in *Coronation Street* (1971), *The New Avengers* (1976-77), *Sapphire and Steel* (1979-80), and most recently *Absolutely Fabulous* (1992-93).

In 1989 Joanna read an abridged version of Ian Fleming's *OHMSS* over 10 nights for BBC Radio 4's series *A Book at Bedtime* and she is now featured on a new series of James Bond spoken word audio tapes. She has also featured in a plethora of lucrative television commercials, both in a voice-over and on-screen capacity and enjoyed much acclaim in a range of theatrical productions.

7. THE AUSTRALIAN GIRL
(Anouska Hempel)

Anouska Hempel's other films include The *Scars of Dracula* (1970) with Jenny Hanley, *Go For A Take* (1972) with Julie Ege, *Tiffany Jones* (1972) and *Double Exposure* (1976). Anouska, or Lady Weinberg as she is also now known, is a successful couturier and owner of the fashionable Blakes Hotel in London.

8. "Please, what is besant"
NANCY (Catherine Von Schell)

Nancy is, like Ruby, one of the more promiscuous among Blofeld's 'Angels of Death'. With the aid of a finger nail file she overrides the electronic locking

system which confines all guests to their quarters, and slips along to Bond's room after dark. He finds her waiting for him on his return from his earlier clandestine meeting with Ruby. Despite our - and Bond's own - momentary concern that he may not be able to rise to the occasion, as we leave the couple, there seems to be little doubt that by morning Nancy will be nothing less than completely satisfied; she is, after all, in the hands of the indefatigable James Bond.

Catherine Von Schell (soon after *OHMSS* she changed her name to the less cumbersome Catherine Schell) was among the Piz Gloria girls given little more to do than simply look decorative. She has since appeared in many other films, including *Moon Zero Two* (1969), *Madame Sin* (1972), *Callan* (1974).

TV appearances more recently include *Clothes In The Wardrobe* (1992).

9. SYLVANNO, the Jamaican girl
(Sylvanna Henriques)

A former Miss Jamaica, Sylvanna also appeared in *The Lost Continent* (1968), during the shooting of which she was badly burned in an accident involving special effects explosives.

10. THE GERMAN GIRL (Ingrid Black)

Before appearing in *OHMSS*, German-born Ingrid appeared in three German-based film productions, though nothing is known of her work since.

11. DENISE, the Israeli girl
(Helena Ronee)

Another German-born actress, Helena also appeared in *The Adventurers* (1970) directed by Lewis Gilbert.

12. THE AMERICAN GIRL
(Dani Sheridan)

Born in Great Britain, Dani also appeared in the films *The Sorcerers* (1967) with Boris Karloff, and *The Brides of Fu Manchu* (1966).

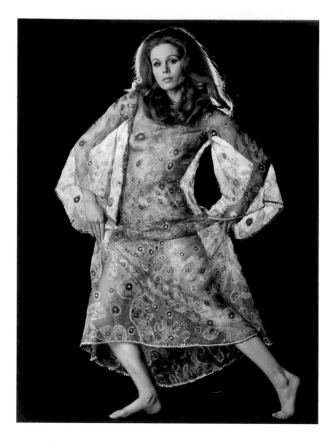

The prickly but rather lovely dress with jewelled knickers. I clearly thought they were only going to use the top half of the photograph, hence sad leg-positioning.

Andrew Sinclair's best selling first novel *The Breaking of Bumbo* was made into a film. Richard Warwick, who was unforgettable in Lindsay Anderson's 'If', was cast as Bumbo, a guard's officer who rebelled against the system, and I was his girlfriend Susie. I remember so well the feel of the gauzy see-through dress I wore in one of the scenes, scratchy and be-jewelled, with gem-encrusted pants, and the uneasy feeling of real wrong-doing when I assisted in the demolition of a waxwork of Winston Churchill. Very soon you learn as an actress that you will have to do and say things which are contrary to your beliefs; but you must become the advocate for the character and your job is to inhabit the person and present her as completely as possible. I hated taking my clothes off for bed scenes (I don't know a soul who is happy with their gear off in front of a large crowd of strangers or, worse, friends). We all had to do it, with varying degrees of success. If you had a 'phwoarrr' body, well and good: if you looked like me, polite clearing of throats. We filmed at EMI/MGM at Elstree which was under the control of Bryan Forbes. On the first day of shooting Forbesy gave me a book; he has never stopped reading and being brainy, quite apart from being a fine actor and director. Isn't it strange that actors are only meant to be interested in acting. As soon as you step outside the box and offer opinions on world affairs, literature, engineering, human rights, you are treated with incredulity, as though you have affronted the natural order of things. Jury members are picked at random, and their deliberations have far more serious consequences, but no-one would think of testing them to see if they were fit to pass judgement on the fate of a fellow human being.

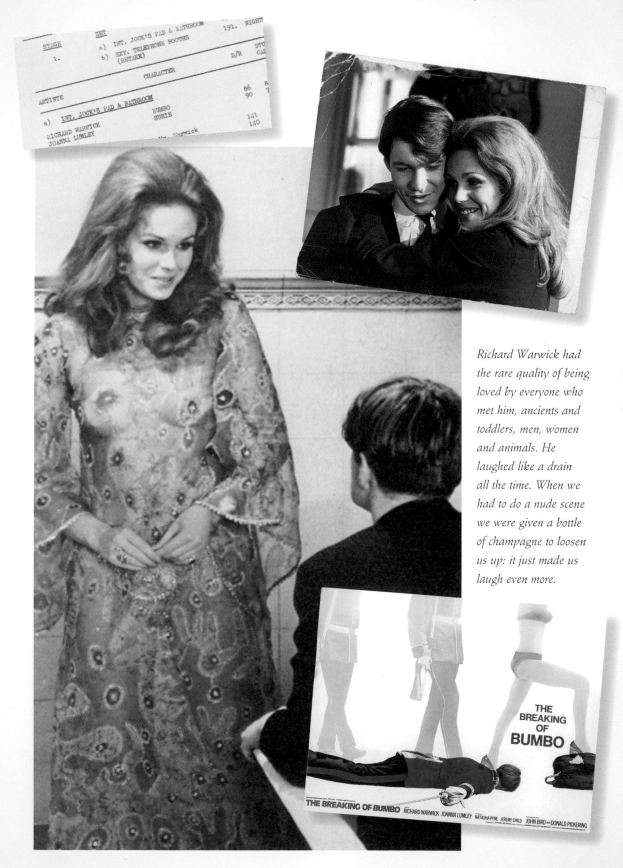

Richard Warwick had
the rare quality of being
loved by everyone who
met him, ancients and
toddlers, men, women
and animals. He
laughed like a drain
all the time. When we
had to do a nude scene
we were given a bottle
of champagne to loosen
us up: it just made us
laugh even more.

93

Ava Gardner was in her early forties when she appeared in the film Tam Lin, directed by Roddy McDowall, in the year when man first landed on the moon. As a latter-day witch she moved amongst a clique of acolytes, fell in love with Ian McShane who in turn was enchanted by Stephanie Beecham playing the local minister's daughter. The film was never released, but it was given all the treatment a star vehicle should have. The costumes of her coven were custom-made; mine included

dresses by Jean Muir and a sensational pink velvet coat by Rupert Lycett Green. The location was Traquair House in Peeblesshire, a small but historically important castle whose famous Bear Gates will never be opened again until a Scottish king is crowned in the British Isles.

Ava, 'Big A' as we called her, was glorious. Ravishingly beautiful, with a handspan waist, she was friendly and approachable; and when she heard I was throwing a party for the minor members of the cast she insisted on turning up at my second-floor rented flat in Addison Road, with her faithful manservant Reggie in attendance carrying a basket of whisky, gin, vodka, tequila, rum and brandy. These she tipped with abandon into a tall china jug and handed out to the guests; shortly after drinking the mixture we could scarcely remember our own names, and the party rocked on until dawn. I thought the world of her: on the first night of the shoot I picked some briar roses for her from the hedgerows and knocked timidly on her door. Her maid let me in and Big A asked me to read Ian McShane's part for the scene she was to shoot the next day. Soon she got tired of rehearsing and, calling for drink ('It tastes better from the bottle'), she asked that the swimming pool in the basement of the sombre Peebles Hydro Hotel be opened so that we could swim. She brought along her dog Cara and her maid Louise and we splashed to and fro as midnight struck. It was whispered that her ex-husband Frank Sinatra still telephoned her every day; theirs was a love that endured all kinds of challenges and rode through all the storms.

The Tam Lin *shoot was dream time: so much hanging around in the soft gardens of Traquair House, so many friends (Michael Billyard-Leake watches me playing 'Moon River' on a mouth organ) and a ravishing wardrobe by Jean Muir. The brown silk jersey and long wool spotted dress were some of many I wore, to be seen only as a glimpse in the background. I have kept all my Jean Muir dresses. They are timeless.*

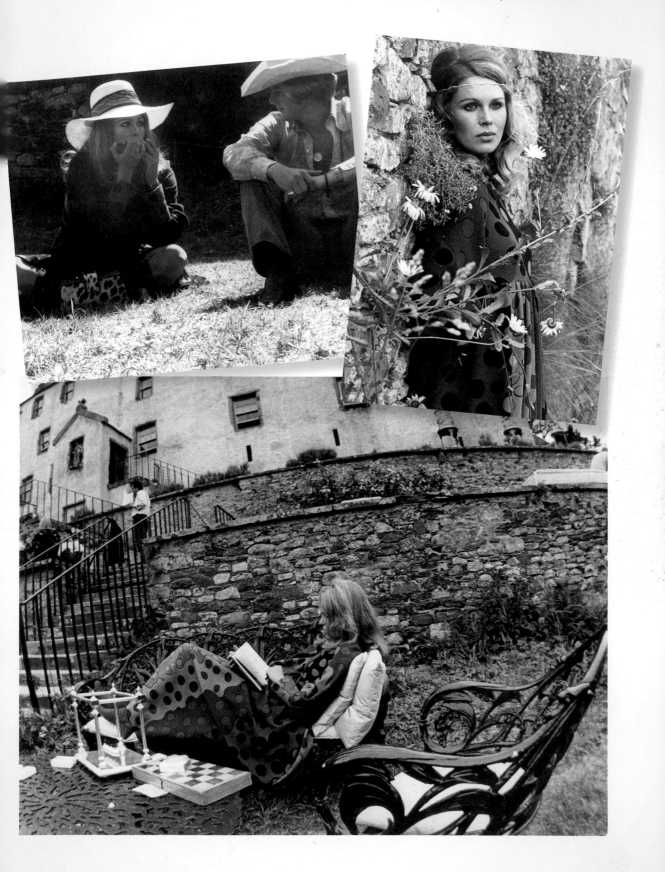

So I was in films: but what about television? How could I get into that world? A television drama called *The Mark 2 Wife* nearly brought an early end to my short and scrappy acting career. I cannot remember being more afraid. My part was tiny, but to make it worse it came right at the end of the play, which was performed almost as if it were on stage, with takes lasting fourteen minutes. I had hardly been called to rehearse as my part was so pitifully small (but all important: I WAS the Mark 2 Wife), and as the moment came for me to swing open the front door and arrive during a monumental marital tiff, in a silver crochet dress with my heart beating louder than a ship's engine... well, I thought I might as well pack it in, as nothing could be worth such agonising torture. From that terrifying experience I have learnt something: be utterly prepared, and hang around watching everything everybody else is doing, and listen to what the actors are saying so that when your words come out you sound at least as though you are on the same planet. Fear has always been my greatest enemy. I know that if you can get that tyrant tamed you are due for a happy life. Easier said than done.

Was it necessary to sit on a roof in a pair of shorts? Yes, if you were publicizing a play in Canterbury; the size of the cathedral forced me up to the chimney-pots to be in the same shot. The hot pants, as they were called, were made by cutting the legs off a pair of men's trousers. Biba boots, in suede, £12 a pair. Even then that was cheap as chips.

So I was in television: but how now to get into the theatre? Having lived my adult life by bluffing or blagging my way into things (pretending I knew what 'blocking' meant, or what it was to 'hit your marks' or even what 'calling the half' and 'get an inky-dink and kill the brute' referred to) I trooped along to the audition for *Not Now Darling* to play a titchy part as a secretary who had two lines in the first scene and one in the last. I didn't know where the 'prompt corner' was, didn't even know what 'upstage' and 'downstage' meant, but you learn fast. Needs must when the devil drives. The play was in repertory at Canterbury: soon after that I trod the London boards at the Garrick Theatre in a Michael Pertwee farce, starring Brian Rix and Alfred Marks, called *Don't Just Lie There, Say Something*. The feeling of walking up the Charing Cross Road and into the stage door, saying hello to the stage doorman and opening your dressing room door with a key, putting your bag down amidst all the familiar make-up and good luck cards, starting to get ready, chit-chattering with fellow actors... I thought this is the business for me. The play was later made into a film with a slight recast; Leslie Phillips took over from Alfred, but the film's budget was lower than a basement window and I don't recall seeing it in any of the big cinemas. No matter: work was work and everything was grist to the mill.

Anyway, my life had changed forever and for the better by the arrival of my little son Jamie. His father, the photographer Michael Claydon, and I never married, but have remained in the closest contact all through Jamie's upbringing and will do always. To be responsible for the most treasured creature on earth is a privilege known to millions of parents the world over, but I guess each time a child is born a bit of extra magic comes your way. Jamie was born in 1967 and he gave a new and proper purpose to my life; from that day on, his welfare became my overriding concern, and work, how to keep the wolf from the door, would be the prime target on my safari.

Farces often include cupboards, plain clothes policemen and mistaken identity. Here Brian Rix, Leslie Phillips and I try to explain our dilemma to Peter Bland, thereby displaying all three elements.

When you see pictures like this one of Leslie and me, it isn't us acting: it is us being directed from behind the camera. Below, however, we are reacting with horror to the arrival of the policeman. Or the politician's wife. Or a hippy with a spray can. I can't remember the details but the writer Michael Pertwee was at the top of his game.

Opposite: my beautiful 1949 Silver Wraith Rolls Royce, with Lucas headlamps and a kneeling Spirit of Ecstasy. She was maroon and black and as lovely as a mid-summer morn.

Elizabeth Knight, Jane Carr, Jennifer Croxton and me in the sitcom Jilly Cooper wrote. Jane had been Mary McGregor in The Prime of Miss Jean Brodie *and knew Maggie Smith, so she was halfway to the stars already.*

The sixties turned into the seventies. Regardless of the dull echo of an empty bank account I borrowed two hundred pounds from my reckless Aunt Joan Mary (she and my mother, when faced with a ludicrously inappropriate adventure, would always say 'Oh DO!') and added it to my last three hundred to buy a beautiful wreck of a Rolls Royce without ever having driven it. When I did, I found the immense vehicle had no working brakes. As soon as they were fixed I gave lifts to my impecunious friends and fellow actors to Pinewood Studios, or to Kent to stay with my long-suffering parents who loved the car and calmly put up with the stray people and dogs who were brought down to stay. Jilly Cooper, the hugely successful columnist turned novelist, wrote a sit-com called It's *Awfully Bad For Your Eyes Darling* which we recorded at the BBC. It starred (starred!!! we were stars!!!) Jane Carr, Elizabeth Knight, Jennifer Croxton and me. I invited Jane to stay during the six weeks we took to make the series, and she stayed for nine years and became one of my all-time best friends. I was still in the Brian Rix farce at the Garrick so every time our television show was aired the announcer was obliged to say 'Miss Lumley is appearing in...', a custom long-since dropped.

My hair was brown at this stage, dyed by me as ever, and frankly rather beastly. JL and I sit on his blue Rolls Royce: this makes us look like millionaires but we only had one rented flat and £400 in the bank.

Also in the show was Jeremy Lloyd, JL as I called him, a tall and dreadfully funny writer and actor; we had met on a grimly unamusing comedy film the year before, married within weeks and sadly divorced within a year. Maybe we just shouldn't have got married, me in Jamie's christening outfit and a funeral hat, at Chelsea Register Office with four guests on a sunny May day: but I don't regret it for a second and nor, I know, does Jeremy. We have stayed close as the days and decades race by, through remarriages and changes of address, through illness and success; we have somehow kept our vows in part without realising it. When we met we had two Rolls Royces and four hundred pounds between us and, as JL said, we could throw a saddle across the world and ride it through the universe (or words to that effect).

Chelsea, May, sunshine, wedding. We both played fairly silly asses in It's Awfully Bad For Your Eyes, Darling. *JL went on to write* Are You Being Served *and* Allo Allo.

When I was very young I was given a garage, not a doll's house, and my passion was collecting Dinky cars. I loved the look of a car or a tractor, or in fact any wheeled vehicle including and especially my gipsy caravan and the golden coronation coach. My collection didn't survive the journey back from the Far East, as I probably gave them to a school friend, but the memory lingered on. As soon as I was seventeen I took my driving test and failed almost before I started for a) wearing a vast black hat that blocked my all-round vision and b) because I drove over a pavement. I continued to drive with L plates

Top: The Borsalino Rolls and my Mini outside the flat in Addison Road. Cold day: fake fur jacket and hat.

In the New Avengers, Gareth Hunt and I as Gambit and Purdey lean cheerfully on a wrecked car: we had probably just killed someone.

for two years (often on my own: I was never stopped or reprimanded. We had a very louche regard for laws) and passed the test at my second attempt. By the time I bought the beautiful, brakeless, Silver Wraith Rolls Royce I had my second Mini as well; then I saw the film *Borsalino* and sent my Roller to be sprayed cream in the East End for about forty quid, a strange and reckless decision that lowered the already dismal value of the car to just above sea level. When I sold her, a dark day in my life, she fetched just £700. Three weeks later I heard she was being advertised for four times that amount. I've been lucky in my life with the cars I've driven, never luckier than when I appeared on *Top Gear*, tutored by the mysterious Stig, in the Reasonably Priced Car. I had to admit to Jeremy Clarkson that I had sold my red Ferrari (what type? – red) and now drove a Lexus and a Smart Car and he nearly fell off the platform with scorn. To drive faster than you normally dare, to hurtle into corners not believing you can pull the car through the turn, to accelerate when your body is shrieking to brake hard… this is petrol-head boy stuff, although many women have proved themselves not only equal to but faster than their male competitors.

And I still collect toy cars. In Africa they make them from discarded tin cans, very perfectly copied from life. I have a taxi and a Land Rover and a Smart Car too, and a big red American beauty which goes quickly on the floor when you vroom it up. A clown and a duck have joined in, both wind-ups; but I realise I have lost my golden coach forever and will have to wait until the next coronation to get another.

Deranged with fear I managed to become the fastest grandmother on Top Gear, but brainy younger Vorderman still beat me. Being tutored by the Stig was a singular honour: he was very kind and patient and completely hidden by his helmet.

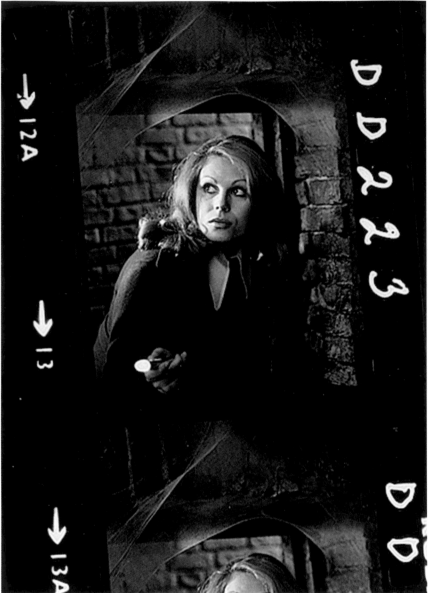

Why would anyone say no to being in a Dracula film, one that starred Peter Cushing as Professor Van Helsing and Christopher Lee as the fanged Count? I said yes at once: my part was Peter's granddaughter Jessica Van Helsing, and the film was released as *The Satanic Rites of Dracula* although we made it under the better title *Dracula is Dead... and Well and Living in London*. (Films often change their titles between shooting and release and quite often you miss seeing them altogether if your eye is not on the ball.) Left alone in a car with strict instructions to stay put Jessica creeps towards a ghastly house in a misty night. 'No Jessica!' you want to yell, 'Don't open that cobwebby creaking door into the cellar, you fool!!' But open it Jess did and saw to her dismay a friendly

Christopher Lee has dominated our screens for decades. I first saw him in The Mummy *when I was still at school: what a thrill to be nearly bitten by him, and then in a later film to play his wife.*

secretary who had been kidnapped and tied to the wall. Valerie Van Ost hung from her manacles uttering piteous cries to release her, and as Jessica approached you wanted to shout 'She's a vampire!!! Look OUT!!' But Jess can't hear you and thick as a plank she tries to untie her friend's bonds. GNASH! The fangs are out and the new vampire lunges at Jess's neck as she backs away in terror. 'Look behind you !!!' we scream but creak the coffins (yes there are coffins there, obviously, it's a cellar) begin to open and out come more bloodsuckers with long nails and very heavy make-up. What's not to like? More important, I made lifelong friends with the frail and marvellous Peter Cushing and dazzlingly accomplished Christopher Lee. Since that film I worked again with Peter in the *New Avengers* and with Christopher in *Boogie Woogie*; it's a weird world when your childhood heroes become your friends.

HAMMER FILM PRODUCTIONS
CALL SHEET   NO: 27

PRODUCTION: "DRACULA IS DEAD...AND WELL...   DATE: Tuesday 19 December 1972
             AND LIVING IN LONDON"   7.00am at studio
LOCATION: Main Car Park   UNIT CALL: 7.15am leave
             Black Park   8.00am on location
             Black Park Road   SCENE NOS:
             Iver   Bucks.
                                                   (1) 79. 82. 83. Day.
SETS: (1) Ext CROXTED HEATH   (2) 49pt. 137. 139. Night.
        (2) Ext GROUNDS, PELHAM HOUSE

DIRECTOR: ALAN GIBSON

ARTIST   CHARACTER   D/R   M/U   ON SET

(1) Ext CROXTED HEATH. 79. 82. 83. Day.
                          MURRAY   9.00am on location
RICHARD COLES   TORRENCE   7.30am on location
WILLIAM FRANKLYN   JESSICA   8.00am on location
JOANNA LUMLEY   COL MATHEWS   7.30am on location
RICHARD VERNON   MOD A   7.30am on location
PAUL JESTON   MOD C   7.30am on location
MARC ZUBER   MOD D   7.30am on location
GRAHAM REES

STAND INS: 7.00am at studio
STUART BARRY for   MR COLES   7.00am at studio
JOHN MOORE for   MR FRANKLYN   7.00am at studio
CAROLINE POOLE for   MISS LUMLEY   7.00am at studio
REG CRANFIELD for   MR VERNON

PROPS: Rifle with telescopic sights, newspaper, pistol for Mod, shoulder
             holster for Torrence.

ACTION VEHICLE: Rover to be on location as arranged.
M/UP: Bullet hole on Mathews' forehead.
SP.FX: Bullet effects. Bullet effect on Torrence.

(2) Ext GROUNDS PELHAM HOUSE. 49pt. 137. 139. Night.
                                               3.30pm on location
CHRISTOPHER LEE   DRACULA   3.00pm on location
PETER CUSHING   LORRIMER   from above
JOANNA LUMLEY   JESSICA
                                               3.00pm on location
STAND INS: from above
GEORGE HOLDCROFT for   MR CUSHING
CAROLINE POOLE for   MISS LUMLEY
ROUTE FROM STUDIO
Turn left from studio via Elstree Station, Aldenham, Hatch End, Eastcote, Ruislip,
Ickenham, Uxbridge, Iver Heath. At Five Points roundabout (Crooked Billet) follow
sign Pinewood studios. Pass studio entrance, follow road to the left and then
first left and first left again. Entrance to car park is immediately left.
The gate is marked "Bucks County Council".

CANTEEN: Meal breaks as arranged with Rank Caterers.

Christopher Lee had Prepare-to-bite and Bite contact lenses, with varying degrees of bloodshot eyeballs. The combination of saturnine beauty and ghastly intentions makes the count irresistible to women; here he looms over Jessica having decided that she will be his bride in the darkness of eternity. My hair was red, the dress a virginal white.

The only time I actually got to set foot in Coronation Street itself: my character Elaine Perkins was deemed too snooty to go to the Rover's Return so all my hopes of a career in Corrie were dashed to smithereens.

Coronation Street came at a time when I needed it most. I was very stretched for cash when I was asked to appear in eight episodes as the new and fleeting love interest in Ken Barlow's life, which had recently been shattered by his wife's electrocution involving a hairdryer. Maybe I would be so compelling that they would write me a permanent part and I could pop into the Rover's Return and get Ken his tea. But they had other better plans for the hero of the street and I was just a distraction for a mad month of his life. He asked me, Elaine Perkins, to marry him but being an idiot I turned him down (I had to; it was in the script) and a month later I was back in London with a clutch of letters I had written to every repertory company in the land asking for a job as an assistant or tea-maker or understudy. Only two replied: no room, not wanted.

*I sit with a posh glass
of sherry while Ken
Barlow tries to excite
me with the prospect of
marriage.*

Something would have to turn up soon, something quite wonderful. It's always darkest before the dawn: but those nights were very black and there was no moon. Just keep on keeping on: make lists and do small things, always look your best, pretend it's all such fun and moan with other actors about the state of the business when inside a little voice is saying 'Do you think you are cut out for this? Are you good enough? Why would anyone want you?' Accept everything that comes along, stay in the boat, try to reach the bank as the current drags you off course again… something will turn up soon.

And then something did.

In The End of Me Old Cigar *at Greenwich Theatre; I spoke only one line in the play, but had the unfading honour of working with Jill Bennett, Rachel Roberts and Keith Barron, and of meeting the great John Osborne who wrote the play which was a resounding flop. I am in the middle, next to Rachel, with nearly black hair and a tattoo on my arm.*

Opposite; having jumped from a blazing building, face attractively sooty, I broke my leg and a surgeon's heart in General Hospital *for six episodes.*

The Big Break

After it had been off air for ten years, it was decided to resurrect *The Avengers*, the massively popular adventure series which had teamed Honor Blackman with Patrick Macnee as partners in fighting crime. They had out-smarted super-sleuths, out-manoeuvred spy-busters and became general saviours of the world. Honor had been succeeded by Diana Rigg, whose universal appeal launched the show to the United States, and after her by Linda Thorson. The show pre-dated the Bond films by a year, and was the first to present a woman as equally tough and cool as a man. It was the most British of productions; Patrick Macnee, immaculate as the quintessential Englishman with a bowler hat and umbrella, was matched in elegance and wit by his leather-clad lady-friend. However, neither the BBC nor ITV wanted to back the revival, and so French money was sought.

The hunt was on for the new Avenger girl, and at the same time for a new male partner for Steed; it was felt that the action should be handled by a younger man, so that Macnee could remain aloof from physical skirmishes. Tremendous excitement and speculation followed the casting process: two or three hundred hopefuls went up for the new parts but no-one was chosen, although a shortlist began to emerge. After a tussle to get into the queue, I finally met the three producers, Albert Fennell, Brian Clemens, who wrote the shows, and Laurie Johnson, composer of the unforgettable theme music. They were singularly unimpressed by what I had done in my short and undistinguished career, and I had to beg them to give me a screen test to prove what I felt in my bones, that this part was mine, was meant for me. Times were as hard as granite as far as work was concerned: I had been lucky enough to get a modelling trip in Italy for a clothes catalogue, but the wolf was at the door and was waving his latch-key. Desperation made me bold: I MUST do a screen test for them, I would

Opposite: in the second series of the New Avengers *my hair was longer: Albert Fennell, our producer, said mournfully that it was fatal to change hairstyles in the middle of a series but I was conscious of how many Purdey haircuts there were around, and wanted to ring the changes. These pictures were shot in France: Jillie Murphy was the stylist and wardrobe mistress.*

ACTA

AGENCY COUNTERING THE AVENGERS

TOP SECRET

OFFICIAL DOSSIER ON

THE NEW AVENGERS

NOTES: This Dossier has A2 Security Rating and in case of enemy attack must be eaten rather than surrendered.

TOP SECRET

A file card taken from The New Avengers HQ.

CODE NAME: PURDEY

The New Avengers

Born Joanna Lumley

Date Undisclosed, India

Early Childhood Travelled in India, Hong Kong and Malaya with Gurka Major father.

Schooling International education including spell at Le Sorbonne, France.

Teens Ambition of becoming surgeon, horse rider, prime minister or ballerina (too tall).

Career Travelled widely (including Moscow) as successful fashion and photographic model. Acting.

Since Recruited by agent John Steed as second member of The New Avengers Team.

Description Height: 1,73 m Figure: 864-609-889 mm (34-24-35).

Drives MGB red white and blue.

Miscellaneous Deceptive, lithesome, eye-catching good looks, expert shot, deadly accurate high-jumping kick. Well versed in all forms of unarmed combat. Disguise a specialty. Fashion fiend.

show them that I was the girl they were looking for. Gareth Hunt, on the short list for the new male role, was to be teamed up with me; I flew back from Italy for a day at my own expense (ouch) to act out a scene with action and dialogue. It was a gruelling and exciting day; but as evening fell they said they would have to look at the work of all the other contenders before they could make any decisions. It felt bad: if they wanted me, wouldn't they say right now? The next day I flew back to Italy to continue the photographic shoot, my spirits at zero. I had hardly stumbled into my hotel room in Amalfi when the phone rang. 'Sit down', said my agent Denis Sellinger, 'You've got the part'. Can I describe what it was like to hear those words? It felt as though

Above: the leotard and tights are spot-on but a blazing disregard for Purdey's face and hair made this doll almost unsaleable.

Opposite: on Purdey's file card it shows her driving an MGB: in fact, I had a rather tricky yellow TR7 with no power steering: it was like a tank to park.

Incredibly flimsy dress, and high heeled shoes which had to be taped onto my feet if I was sprinting or shinning over walls. The heavy Purdey fringe annoyed our lighting cameraman because my eyes were often in shadow.

119

The New Avengers

The black stockings (opposite) conceal my bruised shins, but although Gareth and I took a fair amount of battering during filming the fights and stunts we never broke limbs.

The day of our launch; as requested, the press photographed me in stolen stockings and suspenders, with a gun sensibly tucked into the stocking-top, which is one of an unmatched pair. Rolls Royce again, but this time with Steed's bowler and umbrella.

vast tectonic plates had suddenly slid sideways, as though I could hear the faraway screech and clang of their underground movement and I knew my life was going to change forever from that moment on. I waved farewell to the kind and generous modelling world for good, said goodbye to my familiar life of anonymity and stepped into a different way of being; a situation where I would be paid regularly, where I would work with the cream of British actors every day, where I would make the equivalent of thirteen feature films a year, and become as fit as a flea…where I would become 'famous'.

Gareth had been cast as Mike Gambit, and I was to be Charlie (or 'Charley'); I asked to change the name, as there was a fragrance on the market at the same time called Charlie and I thought we could do better, so I became Purdey, named after a model and the superb shotgun. It was essential that we were trained to be as fit as possible in a very short time, so Gareth and I were up before dawn every day to undertake a rigorous routine of shuttle runs, push-ups, sit-ups,

The New Avengers

The New Avengers

The New Avengers

We did the publicity shots during our lunch hours when we were also interviewed for magazines, fitted for clothes and in my case taught to tap-dance (15 minutes allowed) and ride a motor bike (25 minutes and that's your lot). I funked the bike riding and got a stuntman in a wig to do it.

stretching and, in my case, sobbing for mercy. Gradually we became super-fit, limber and supple, fast and strong. There was much talk about Purdey's wardrobe: should she still be in leather, or in girly-gear, as we had two men already? Dresses and high-heels it was, and stockings and suspenders, which rather appalled me as I had hoped to present her as a tomboy. May I cut my shoulder length hair? Certainly not; whoever heard of a heroine with short hair. Oh please...and I did, and it was fine, more than fine, terrific (and tomboyish).

Before I had it cut (by an improbably handsome young hairdresser called John Frieda, assisted by a beautiful red-haired boy called Nicky Clarke) we had to announce the news to the press at an early morning photocall at the Dorchester Hotel in London. On the morning, just after 8 o'clock, dressed in my floaty clothes and a big smile, I was taken aback to find that unless I flashed my stocking tops the newspapers wouldn't print a single picture. But what were we going to do; I was wearing tights, and the shops weren't open. We walked into the Dorchester Hotel, found a middle-aged woman, frog-marched her to the Ladies' Room, tore off her stockings and suspenders, probably gave her a fiver for her trouble (and trauma), and then, dressed correctly for the press, I returned in the nick of time, with a revolver tucked into my stocking-top; the press sighed with relief. It was only after the event as I took the stockings off that I saw that they were not a pair.

Because Purdey had trained as a dancer her high kick was lethal, particularly to saps who dared to think that she was a bit girlie because of Flimsy Dress (see p119).

Pinewood Studios was the backdrop for many episodes, doubling as a stately home, a laboratory, a Ministry of Defence building and, in one episode, China. When the three Avengers drove together, Purdey always ended up in the cramped back seat, like a nodding dog in the rear window.

Fight days were my favourites: stunt men and women are my heroes in the industry because they are so incredibly disciplined, brave and accurate. Our action director Ray Austin, once a stuntman himself, taught me to run, kick, punch, fall, roll, climb, spin a car, fire a gun…and how not to moan even when things were grim. Over the page, Purdey protects an incriminating hand-print on the top of an old car. Going though the carwash, ordinary cold water jetting like cannons, being covered with buckets of detergent for comic effect on a freezing cold November day in Canada was something I will never forget. There was nowhere for me to rinse off the slimy suds: so the car wash was cleared and I stood in my underwear with power jets turned full on. Avengers never complain.

3154

I could not have loved my two years on the *New Avengers* more. Patrick, Gareth and I became firm friends for life: we worked so hard we were giddy and exhausted, but I got to do many of my own stunts and to work with the best of the best. The money was not terrific, and I didn't manage to struggle out of debt for years to come, but my undying gratitude to the producers and actors has never dimmed.

In the publicity we had to do, day after day, for publications around the world, I found that my real life had somehow been blended in with Purdey's rather racier background. (As a public figure, you have to get used to stories appearing which are complete fabrication and this was good training.) Suddenly I acquired a university education, at the Sorbonne, no less: and my father, in one version, had been a bishop who was shot as a spy. No matter; the pleasant lie that I grew too tall for the Royal Ballet has put me in good stead all my life. Each week the New Avengers saved the world as we overcame all obstacles, taking us to France and Canada, as the programme was re-financed further and further afield. The *New Avengers* had not only saved the world: they had saved me too.

Patrick Lichfield and Terry O'Neill took wonderful pictures of us all. The one on the far right is my favourite of Purdey: sensible jeans, but made a bit cheeky by not wearing anything under the flying jacket: hair not looking too pudding-y and a name on the helmet in case you forgot who she was. Stare down the barrel of the lens: that's the trick.

Bruce Oldfield made Sapphire's dress with light blue buttons on dark blue silk jersey.

David McCallum, the heart-throb Illya Kuryakin from *The Man from Uncle*, and I became *Sapphire and Steel* a year after the *New Avengers* had ridden into the sunset. As Sapphire, I could stop time with my alien skills and flashing blue-lensed eyes, and Steel, with his extra-terrestrial mega-brain, sorted out the evil that stalked our planet. For the next two years we worked in a dark studio with special effects and eerie, thrilling stories that scared our young audience. P. J. Hammond, the writer, had tapped into a vein of uneasy fiction where children vanished from photographs to re-appear in real life as grey wraiths, and a dead soldier of the Great War haunted a railway station where he had said his last goodbye before being killed. Some of the stories tested the notion of time past and present; with McCallum and our clever directors applying their incisive deductive powers we steered a path of logic through a complex web of intrigue. Sapphire wore blue clothes of strange and unfashionable design, because she was an alien and had no idea of, or interest in, the fashion of the day. She and Steel looked vaguely normal, although Steel was unable to behave like a human as he had no emotions and no empathy with the people he had come to help. There was a children's television comic called Look-In: if you did look in, and thousands did, you would have seen us as a cartoon strip. It is very gratifying to be drawn as a cartoon character. I have kept a pile of the comics, and also an original front cover which depicts Mork and Mindy before Robin Williams became a movie star, Bob Geldof in his Boomtown Rats era, Christopher Reeve as Superman and us: a portrait of the favourite heroes of the time.

McCallum's dazzling good looks have never faded. My hair grew from shortish to long over the two years we shot the show.

131

The railway platform was so realistically made in the studio that people wrote in to say they knew the village where we had shot it. Sapphire became the schoolmistress the young soldier had longed to see again.

I was pleased to get my hands on a wig once in a while.

*Richard Mulligan had
to age up mightily to
play the doddering
father of Inspector
Clouseau: my character
Marie Jouvert was
trying to trace the
elusive and bungling
detective, unforgettably
created by Peter Sellers.*

Quick and fast the work came tumbling in. Two *Pink Panther* films shot at the same time, with me playing a different part in each, allowed me to meet and work with giants of the cinema, Blake Edwards, Herbert Lom and Bert Kwouk, Capucine and the immortal David Niven, but not, alas, Peter Sellers who had died previously. The budgets were huge, but the planning of the locations was sketchy and a lot of money was wasted as we flew to and fro across Europe, coming to rest occasionally like birds of passage only to take off again before a foot of film was shot. Do you remember the ground-breaking US comedy show called *Soap*? Richard Mulligan starred in it, and became a firm favourite in the UK. To work with him, playing Clouseau's old father, was to know hysterical laughter, stifled between teeth until Blake croaked 'Cut!' and we wiped away tears of mirth. It was a strange time though, threaded through with a sense of 'don't care if it succeeds or not', not the best way to approach film-making. I went on a long and exciting promotional tour of the United States, Canada, France and Spain but the films were not a success. (I have just remembered: I was so impatient with the debate before shooting about how my hair should look that I went home and hacked it off myself, so that there could be no further talk. I shall not do that again. Or: maybe I will. I always snip away at my hair, and dye it myself, partly out of boredom with the way I look, and partly because I think I am at heart a failed crimper.)

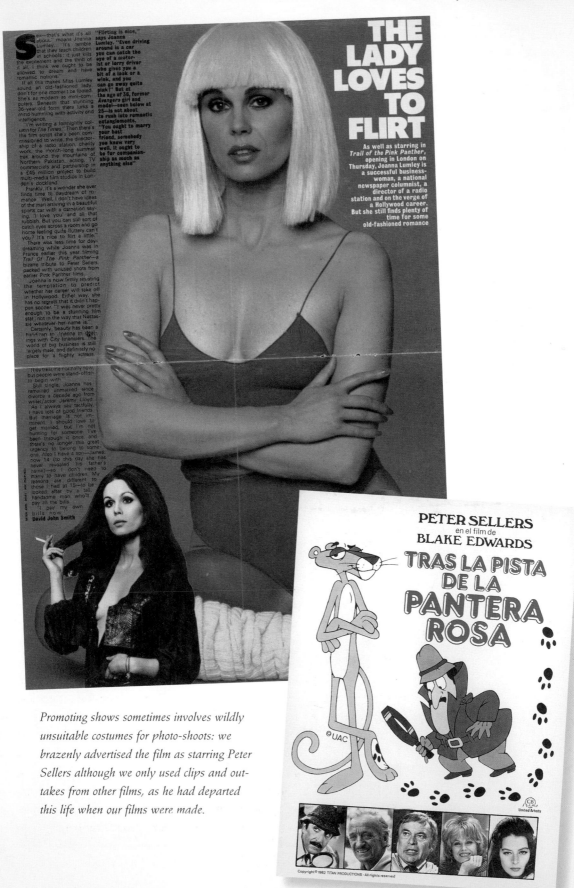

THE LADY LOVES TO FLIRT

As well as starring in *Trail of the Pink Panther*, opening in London on Thursday, Joanna Lumley is a successful business-woman, a national newspaper columnist, a director of a radio station and on the verge of a Hollywood career. But she still finds plenty of time for some old-fashioned romance

Sex—that's what it's all about," moans Joanna Lumley. "It's terrible that they teach children in schools; it just kills the excitement and the thrill of it all. I think we ought to be allowed to dream and have romantic notions."

If all this makes Miss Lumley sound an old-fashioned lady, don't for one moment be fooled. She's as modern as mini-computers. Beneath that stunning 36-year-old form there lurks a mind humming with activity and intelligence.

"I'm writing a fortnightly column for *The Times*. Then there's the film script she's been commissioned to write, the directorship of a radio station, charity work, the month-long summer trek around the mountains of Northern Pakistan, acting, TV commercials and partnership in a £45 million project to build multi-media film studios in London's dockland.

Frankly, it's a wonder she ever finds time to daydream of romance. Well, I don't have ideas of the man arriving in a beautiful sports car with a carnation saying, 'I love you' and all that rubbish. But you can sail sort of catch eyes across a room and go home feeling quite fluttery can't you? It's nice to flirt a little."

There was less time for daydreaming while Joanna was in France earlier this year filming *Trail Of The Pink Panther*—a bizarre tribute to Peter Sellers, packed with unused shots from earlier Pink Panther films.

Joanna is now firmly resisting the temptation to predict whether her career will take off in Hollywood. Either way, she has no regrets that it didn't happen sooner. "I was never pretty enough to be a stunning film star, not in the way that Nastassia whatever-her-name is."

Certainly, beauty has been a handicap to Joanna in dealings with City financiers. The world of big business is still largely male, and definitely no place for a flighty actress.

"They treat me normally now, but people were stand-offish to begin with."

Still single, Joanna has remained unmarried since divorce a decade ago from writer/actor Jeremy Lloyd. "As I always say tactfully, I have lots of good friends. But marriage is not imminent. I should love to get married, but I'm not hunting for someone. I've been through it once, and there's no longer this great urgency to belong to someone. Also I have a son—James, now 14 (to this day she has never revealed his father's name)—so I don't need to marry to have children. My reasons are different to those I had at 18—to be looked after by a tall, handsome man who'll pay all the bills."

"I pay my own bills now."

David John Smith

"Flirting is nice," says Joanna Lumley. "Even driving around in a car you can catch the eye of a motor-ist or lorry driver who gives you a bit of a look or a wink, and you can go away quite pink!" But at the age of 36, former *Avengers* girl and model—seen below at 25—is not about to rush into romantic entanglements.

"You ought to marry your best friend, somebody you knew very well. It ought to be for companionship as much as anything else"

PETER SELLERS
en el film de
BLAKE EDWARDS

TRAS LA PISTA DE LA PANTERA ROSA

© UAC

United Artists

Promoting shows sometimes involves wildly unsuitable costumes for photo-shoots: we brazenly advertised the film as starring Peter Sellers although we only used clips and out-takes from other films, as he had departed this life when our films were made.

Sun exclusive on one of the most beautiful women in Britain

MEN, MARRIAGE AND ME—BY MISS PINK PANTHER

BIZARRE BONUS BY JOHN BLAKE

HER eyes are the soft azure blue of the Caribbean. Her legs stretch on for ever.

She is brilliant, witty, rich, eminently desirable and instantly recognised wherever she goes.

Face to face, Joanna Lumley is, quite simply, one of the most beautiful women I have ever met.

Already her glittering TV roles in The New Avengers and Sapphire And Steel have turned her into every thinking man's number one sex symbol.

Now she gets big-screen star billing as the heroine of a new Pink Panther movie.

The film, Trail Of The Pink Panther, has been created around off-cuts from films made by Peter Sellers before his untimely death. It opens in London next week.

And yet, at a time when she should be showering the world with champagne bubbles, Joanna quietly admits that there is a huge gap in her life.

At 36, after love affairs with Rod Stewart and actor Michael Kitchen plus a madcap two-week marriage to actor Jeremy Lloyd, Joanna now has no man in her life.

Yes, she says wistfully. "I think I probably would like to be married—very much.

Steady

"But you can't just get married. It takes two, you know. So you don't just wed the state, you don't just want to be married.

"You want to be with someone who appears to you to be the best company possible for the rest of your life.

"It's quite a step and I think it probably grows harder to take as you grow older, for several reasons.

"One of the biggest things is that you are more independent, simply because you have grown up for longer."

Not surprisingly Joanna has had numerous proposals, both from steady

'I have had quite a few proposals'

boyfriends and from men she has never met.

"But you must remember that when you marry someone you have to be in love with them, they must be in love with you, you must want to marry them and they must want to marry you," she says.

"All those things come together pretty rarely, which is why most people only marry once or twice in a lifetime.

"Just because a whole lot of people have proposed to me doesn't mean that any of them was right for me.

"I'm really not sure how many proposals I have had but there have been quite a few.

"Many of them were from people I've never met.

"I'm quite certain that most of these proposals were honestly meant.

"Quite often I was sent very beautiful letters from people who were lonely.

"I think some of them saw in Purdy, the charac-

School

ter I played in the New Avengers, someone they thought they wanted to marry because she seemed to be so strong and so organised.

"But Purdy wasn't really me, of course.

"I don't live sipping champagne from a flute-stemmed glass.

"In fact, I'm so ordinary I'm stunningly ordinary. I forget to shop, I cut the fat off cheese and I do all the ordinary things that any ordinary housewife has to do."

Much of Joanna's time now is spent looking after her 15-year-old son Jamie, who is a pupil at Harrow School.

He was born before Joanna married but she refuses to say who the father is.

"I never talk about him in interviews because they take the papers at his school," she says.

"When he's 18 he can say whatever he wants to

say himself, but it's not really fair for me to talk about him now."

Yet Joanna's eyes sparkle whenever she talks about her son.

"He's a good friend as well as a son," she says.

Recently the two of them went together on a holiday to Pakistan with a group who were studying the traditions of the Ismaili people.

Absurd

"I think the trip came at just the right time for me," she says.

"It gave me time to think, which is something I don't usually have.

"And it also let me think about the things that I must remember now that the Pink Panther film is about to be released.

"Because the things that might well be coming my way soon because of it are very seductive—large sums of money, great fame, it's all absurd.

"But being out there among the people living in the mountains of Pakistan reminded me that being rich and famous is not the be-all and end-all of life.

"What is really important is ordinary things like family, friends and health.

Yachts

"I live in a little flat in Holland Park, London. I drive a tiny Renault Five and that's

WIN FABULOUS DIAMOND RINGS

★ THE PINK Panther is the name of the priceless diamond stolen in the Peter Sellers, Joanna Lumley film Trail Of The Pink Panther.

annually to a maximum of 50 per cent of the original price.

That means in five years' time each ring will have increased its trade-in value to £150—the price at which Zales

The 'rinky-dink' panther himself appeared from time to time in a full furry costume which luckily I never had to wear.

Make-up checks before a take: it looks as though my head has been lowered onto my shoulders. Dress by Jean Muir.

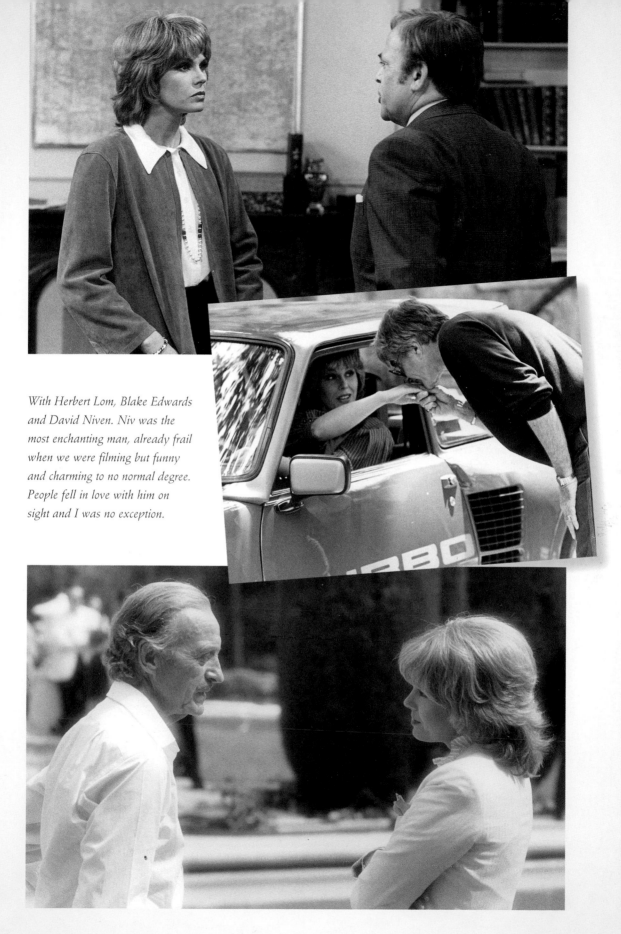

With Herbert Lom, Blake Edwards and David Niven. Niv was the most enchanting man, already frail when we were filming but funny and charming to no normal degree. People fell in love with him on sight and I was no exception.

This is the Life

Most actors I know always want to be in something they're not: for instance, when doing a film you long for the thrill of the stage, and yet when you are pitching up to do a comedy before a sparsely-filled house on tour, you think: Oh for the television studios and the fun of a shared trailer! And so it goes on, the grass always appearing greener somewhere else. If you are lucky, you can duck and dive between them all, with the odd radio play and a commercial or two, some lovely voice-overs and the huge treat of a documentary in faraway lands. More by good luck than design, more from necessity than clever planning, I have found myself changing horses time and again, and I am endlessly thankful for the vast variety of work I have been able to do. You become a sort of jack-of-many-trades (and master of none) and, keeping in mind the old military adage 'Always present a moving target', you can escape real catastrophes by flitting on to the next job before you are gunned down and grounded. Even when you are praised to the skies you have an uneasy feeling that you will be 'found out'; no actors rest upon their laurels. Inside ourselves, we know when we have done reasonable work and we are always trying to improve our art. This often means taking on dubious projects which you think are interesting but turn out to be dire. I just love working; pretending to be other people is an endlessly rewarding, and sometimes rather pointless, way of spending your life. But once in a while, when the theatre audience holds its breath, or the cinema gasps with terror, or the studio breaks down in hysterical laughter, the whole profession seems like the most agreeable occupation on earth. It's story telling, plain and simple; and I am as happy to be in the audience as on stage or screen, if the story is well told.

There is a different way of performing, for the screen or the live stage; but at the heart of it you have to believe utterly in what you are saying or doing, whether it is comedy, drama or tragedy. You have to minimise your expression if the camera is only three feet away from your face, and yet be able to show by your whole body what you are thinking when the live audience is two thousand strong. On film, you can try again if the first, or twelfth, take is no good, but in the theatre you have only one crack at it per performance, with the added advantage of having rehearsed the scene for a month or more beforehand. Part of the skill is saying lines after eight months, eight shows a week, as though they had just come into your head, keeping them as fresh as a mouthful of mint. During the long hours on a film set, when you haven't been used all day and you thought your scene was hugely important, you must be able to step up to the plate at 5.20 pm and deliver the lines in one take, with your back to the camera, because time has run out: and you won't get the reverse shot in which you thought you could show you were a match for Meryl Streep. 'Expect nothing' is what I have learnt; if there were any certainties in our game we would all be millionaires. Even if you cast the top talent with a blindingly good script, and throw money at it, there is no guarantee that you will have a hit. Like gambling, it's the not-knowing that keeps you as keen today as you were when you were a starry-eyed beginner.

I seldom watch the work I have done when the shoot is over. (In the theatre, of course, you can never see yourself, and must rely on friends and critics to let you know how you were.) Occasionally I have

Greg Hicks as a revolutionary in the stage play Vanilla, *by Jane Stanton Hitchcock and directed by Harold Pinter. My part was Miralda Sumac, a murderous dictatrix who comes to a bad end. The play, though very funny, was not well received. The gold gloves, here being inched off by Greg, are upstairs in my drawer as I write. I keep things.*

come across something I had filmed many years before and had rather swept under my mind's carpet for fear of it being shaming: but lo and behold, it wasn't so bad, was actually rather good.

But I remember it all; the beating heart and shaking hands before the first night, the attempts at accents with varying degrees of success, the shared sense of elation when the curtain falls to a thunder of applause, the vague sense of disappointment when some great star doesn't turn out to be as charming as you had hoped they would be, costumes you could hardly breathe in, heated disputes about the location caterers, the remaining wig-glue that you continue to pick off during dinner at grand restaurants in town. So much effort goes on to make a night at the theatre, or an evening in front of a series on television, something memorable or pleasing…and then pfff! like a mist rolling off the sea it's gone, and people stretch their legs and say: 'Where shall we eat?' and all your hard work has gone, has done its job. But oh! the friends you make! and the tales you can tell. Was it the fox in *Pinocchio* who sang 'Hey diddley-dee, an actor's life for me?' I think so: I am with the fox.

Simon Cadell and I worked in three Noel Coward plays together: he was as good an actor as you can get, able to switch effortlessly between comedy and full-on drama. David Shilling, the famous hat-maker, made my lovely white silk brocade dress for me.

*As Anthony Perkins'
girlfriend in* The Glory
Boys. *It was exciting
to work with two actors
I admired so much:
he and Rod Steiger,
however, didn't hit it
off and Perkins actually
measured Steiger's
caravan to see if it was
larger than his.*

143

Peter Rice designs glorious clothes for theatre and opera; it is always a privilege to be squished into corsets for a creation that you know is going to look magnificent on stage. 'Il faut souffrir pour etre belle': you must suffer to be beautiful. Wicked Mrs Cheveley wearing a heliotrope dress in Oscar Wilde's play An Ideal Husband; David Gwillum as Sir Robert Chiltern knows he is dealing with a minx.

145

We all thought Vanilla was terribly funny but the audience stayed away in droves. Just as we were about to close, Time Out *said it was the funniest show in town, but it was too late to save us. The cast was so high-powered that all our names appeared above the title.*

With Gwen Humble, Charlotte Cornwell, Sian Phillips and Ron Cook. Hair cut by me and dyed pitch black, courtesy of a high-street chemist.

146

Lovejoy *with the evergreen Ian McShane. Nice to work with him again so long after* Tam Lin. *I had been sprayed light brown to match him and to show that I came from South America.*

Jerry Hall as Miss Scarlet in a small TV series called Cluedo which
disappeared too soon. It was hosted by Richard Madeley, and hauled in lovely
people to play the well-known characters from the board game. I was Mrs
Peacock, Nicholas Parsons was the Reverend Green: Liz Smith was Mrs White,
John Bird was Professor Plum and Leslie Grantham cast aside the shades of
Dirty Den to play Colonel Mustard.

149

Class Act

CARLTON UK
Television

We had such a happy time making Class Act, John Bowe, Nadine Garner and I: Verity Lambert produced the series and insisted we use her splendid Great Dane Arthur Daley in the show. He mostly did what he wanted, sometimes ambling along behind Richard Vernon, who played my father, sometimes walking off the set before the director yelled 'Cut!' The duck was treated very kindly and respectfully, and caring for her well-being and small foibles put hours onto already long days. It was a very good show and went to a second series; but the restless eyes of the television stations are always looking for the new kid on the block, sometimes elbowing the old kid out of the picture altogether. Many babies are thrown out with the bathwater.

151

Innocent Lies *started out with a different title.
Oddly, I don't remember very much about this one
except that it starred the excellent Adrian Dunbar,
who had to carry me down a long flight of stairs,
and that fine American actor, Stephen Dorff. He
and Gabrielle Anwar played my children.*

Voicing animated films is an art of its own. You know what your character, or toy, looks like and how it will behave; you record the script like a radio play and the animators work to your sound track. Bob Hoskins was Teddy and I was the rag doll Annie (below right) in The Forgotten Toys; the late great Clement Freud voiced a dog and the multi-talented Andrew Sachs did all the other voices.

COLD COMFORT FARM

January 1st 1995
at 9.30pm on BBC1

Starring
EILEEN ATKINS
KATE BECKINSALE
SHEILA BURRELL
STEPHEN FRY
FREDDIE JONES
JOANNA LUMLEY
IAN McKELLEN
MIRIAM MARGOLYES
RUFUS SEWELL
ANGELA THORNE

Directed by
JOHN SCHLESINGER
Adapted by
MALCOLM BRADBURY
From the novel by
STELLA GIBBONS
Produced by
ALISON GILBY

Photography
CHRIS SEAGER

Production Designer
MALCOLM THORNTON

Film Editor
MARK DAY

Music
ROBERT LOCKHART

Executive Producers
RICHARD BROKE   ANTONY ROOT
(BBC Television)   *(Thames Television)*
A BBC Television/Thames Television
Production

John Schlesinger directed the Stella Gibbons' classic
Cold Comfort Farm *which had a raft of stars in
it. Partly shot in London and then in Sussex meant
that I only worked with Kate Beckinsale who played
the lead, Flora, as my Mrs Smiling only featured in
the London scenes. This often happens in filming;
you pretend later that you rubbed shoulders with the
whole team. And what a team this was.*

155

San Francisco was the location for the Roald Dahl movie James and the Giant
Peach, *partly animated, and produced by Tim Burton and Walt Disney. Miriam
Margolyes and I played Aunt Sponge and Aunt Spiker and had a bad time
being winched up to be spun in a spider's web. Producer Jake Eberts didn't mind
talking to me when I was in Aunt Spiker garb, with cunningly applied prosthetic
make-up to make my lips thinner and my spiteful face crueller.*

Although it wasn't received with cries of joy, *Prince Valiant* provided me with an enviable costume for Morgan Le Fay. The black leather dress and snake circlet were hot in the heat of a Berlin summer where we shot it; I had a stunt double, who was thrown into a cauldron of boiling stew.

*John Schlesinger
directed* Sweeney
Todd *at the Ardmore
Studios outside Dublin;
Ben Kingsley played the
Demon Barber, and as
Mrs Lovett, gruesome
maker of human pies, I
was rigged up in blood-
stained apron and a
shrivelled wig with
scabs in it. I asked John
how he saw my part:
he said 'I think she
has bad teeth', so they
were darkened down
each day. This dark
story was fun to shoot
although Campbell
Scott and I never got to
hold hands as we do in
this publicity picture.*

Mrs Lovett
Sweeney Todd

159

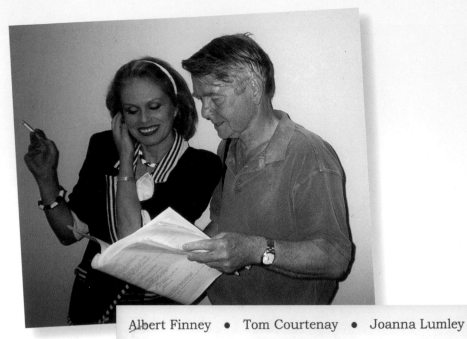

Once in a lifetime your prayers are answered: and when the go-ahead was finally given for the Angela Lambert story A Rather English Marriage to be filmed I knew I had landed in paradise. Albert Finney and Tom Courtenay are simply the best: and more than that, they are the best company you could hope for. I cried when I saw the transmission; at the end the two frail old men danced slowly to 'I'm Going to Get You On a Slow Boat to China' and somehow their enduring friendship in real life blossomed out of the beautiful scene, so sensitively directed by Paul Seed. The clothes were from the eighties, so it was big shoulders and bling jewellery for my pushy, ambitious character.

Albert Finney • Tom Courtenay • Joanna Lumley

A Rather English Marriage

Marriage is a funny thing, ...isn't it?

BBC TWO

160

JOANNA LUMLEY
plays Donna Sinclair

Donna Sinclair is the star of the soap and never lets anyone forget it. She plays Dr Willoughby, a successful, glamorous and compassionate surgeon, but in reality Donna is a neurotic, ageing actress who cares more about her celebrity status than anything else.

Joanna was instantly attracted to the role of Donna Sinclair. "It's terribly rare to read scripts that make you laugh out loud but I thought 'this is paradise' as soon as I read Dr Willoughby," she says.

"I didn't have a shadow of doubt about the role and I wasn't at all concerned about who else they were going to cast. Sometimes you think 'I can do that if we get a big name to play so and so' but I just knew that if they wanted me to play Donna they were on the right track and whoever else they cast would be brilliant."

Asked about the kind of woman Donna Sinclair is, Joanna explains "Donna has muscled her way into the role of Dr Willoughby and she will not let it go. She is very vain and self-regarding and she knows that this is her big slot."

"I think Donna believes that most people in the street are talking about the episode of Dr Willoughby from the day before and that she's a colossal national figure. It is more likely that very few people watch Dr Willoughb[y . . . .] viewers are probably people who are wheeled up in front of it."

"She wears the same kind of clothes all the time – sh[e . . .] because they hide the wrinkles, and clothes that slig[. . .] waistline. I think she wears trim corsetry undernea[th . . .] health farm and she relies on heavy make up."

"In fact, Donna would hate to been seen without h[er . . .] best. I'm not like that, which is one of the reason[s . . .] programme. I knew that after that nobody would [. . .] caught you looking awful' because I have alread[y . . .]

Joanna sported a new look for the part, wearing [. . .] colour myself, in fact I have been every colour [. . .] wigs, one longer than the other, and she preten[ds . . .] has her hair cut. She's getting on a bit and so s[he . . .] and scratches under the wig with a pencil."

JOANNA LUMLEY

Dr Willoughby: A Pearson Television Production for ITV

Picture by Tony Russell

"Donna is also a terrible budget drier. She has go[t . . .] everyone else has to make do with these awful little broom cup[boards . . .] most English actors are terribly grateful in general. There's no point in screaming and saying 'I demand more' because on the budgets they have they often can't give you

/cont'd

Above: Coming Home *and* Nancherrow *followed the story of a family through its adventures and sorrows. Peter O'Toole played my husband and Poppy Gaye played my little daughter. The school-friend she brought back to stay was a 12-year-old Keira Knightley. We could all see that she was going to go far, but I don't think any of us guessed just how far.*

Left: this funny spoof on a daytime TV serial only ran for six episodes. I liked playing Donna, insufferably conceited, who scratched her head under her wig with a pencil.

163

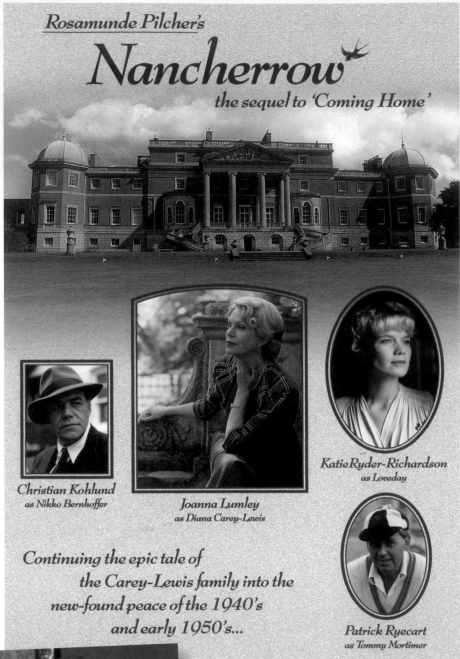

Rosamunde Pilcher's

Nancherrow

the sequel to 'Coming Home'

Christian Kohlund
as Nikko Bernhoffer

Joanna Lumley
as Diana Carey-Lewis

Katie Ryder-Richardson
as Loveday

Patrick Ryecart
as Tommy Mortimer

*Continuing the epic tale of
the Carey-Lewis family into the
new-found peace of the 1940's
and early 1950's...*

Nancherrow *was a very happy series to work on,
and a proud one for me. Patrick Macnee flew in from
Palm Springs, the first and only time I have acted
with him since I called him Steed thirty years before.*

Huge scenes, like cricket matches, dances and weddings take days to shoot, with lots of actors and what we call 'extras', a vital part of all shows, who provide the right colour, style and flavour of the period, and often the skills too. Above, Patrick Ryecart and I execute a shambolic tango amidst a crowd of people who could do it far better.

165

As you get older, so do your 'love interests'. Christian Kohlund and I nearly met decades before when he was squiring one of the Bond girls in Murren. We found plenty to talk about in our romantic scenes together as we sipped our ginger ale masquerading as champagne.

You get to wear a rare hat or two. Our period clothes come from theatrical costumiers, whose vast storage halls are stalked by ghosts of flapping tailshirts and puttees, ball gowns and car-coats of days gone by.

Being Dolly Bantry, Miss Marple's best friend, allowed me to work with two zonking great talents, Geraldine McEwan and Julia Mackenzie. Miss Marple will endure forever, as long as they don't try to modernise her from the quiet, observant, brainy creature that Agatha Christie created. I have started to look like my mother in some of the shots I see in front of me: I like to think that people long departed still watch us and enjoy our efforts to entertain.

Given the whip hand (as I usually am) I can do my own make-up quickly and accurately. Elinor Glyn in The Cat's Meow *had dark red hair and marvellously kohl-rimmed eyes.*

Rachel Stirling + Joely
Maybe Baby   Richardson

Above: I spelt Rachael's name wrong on this polaroid, quite often the only record we have of the work we are in. Lovely to stand between the daughters of two glorious actresses, Diana Rigg and Vanessa Redgrave. The film Maybe Baby *was by Ben Elton and starred Joely and Hugh Laurie. (How were we to know he would become an American idol in* House. *Talented beyond belief. Nicer than pie.)*

Left: Tim Burton gave me this little figure of Maudeline Everglot, a character I voiced in Corpse Bride. *And no, I didn't get to meet Johnny Depp.*

Ermintrude, the opera-mad cow, in The Magic Roundabout. *Vain and yet endearing, I based her voice and attitude on Patricia Routledge as Hyacinth Bucket. Although the film starred Robbie Williams and Kylie Minogue I didn't meet them during the recording. Just as well, the way Ermintrude sang.*

Denis Lawson stole away our hearts as the cool, moody inn-keeper in the film Local Hero. We were cast as husband and wife in Hugo Blick's finely written tragi-comedy Sensitive Skin; our marriage was unravelling, and sometimes it felt so like real life that I wanted to shout at Davina (my character) 'You fool! You're going to lose him!' Playing half of a married couple, or a parent or daughter, involves a new strand of imaginative role-playing: how often do they bicker in the car? What does he find sweet about her? Why can't she talk to him? Will she miss him? Well, yes she did; and when he was gone she fell into the untrustworthy arms of another man, played by Anthony Head, who steered her easily into bed (see below). Regrets? She had a few: but then again too few to mention. Fabulous stuff. Blick is a very, very clever man.

Delilah Stagg only appeared in a few episodes of Jennifer Saunders' bittersweet comedy series Jam and Jerusalem. *I think I liked riding my bike along the street so slowly that I was overtaken by pedestrians as much as anything in the world. JS and I in hats sit amongst the stellar cast.*

To play on Broadway, to be in a show in New York City, was something beyond my wildest dreams. Actually, not even dreams: I didn't even think about it. When it happened to me it was a like being hit by a train. The warmth of the NY audience surged towards us and engulfed us, and David Hirson's extraordinary, wordy, funny play became a bit of a cult hit. Mark Rylance, whose brilliance blazes from everything he touches, brought the house to its feet with every performance as Valere, the shabby wily street clown angling to find a place in the princess's troupe of players, led by the immaculate David Hyde Pierce. At the curtain call of the first preview a bouquet of sixty red roses was shunted across the stage bearing the message 'Joanna – Welcome to Broadway!'. The card stayed on my dressing-room mirror until the show closed four months later, in a flurry of snow and the dark days of winter in that beautiful city. I brought the princess's two little dolls back to live with me at home: the princess liked them to swing from her skirt so she had something to fiddle with when she was muddled or angry.

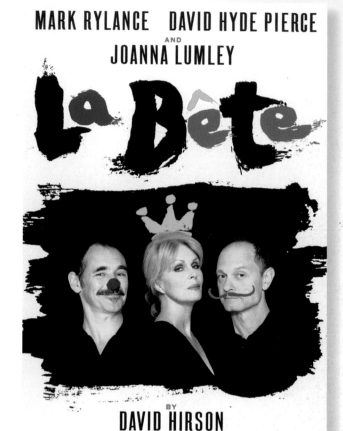

VALERE

Well Heaven Bless Us! NOW I see
It was a sudden burst of piety
That took you from the table, am I right?
I'm so relieved! I though, perhaps, your flight
Was caused by something I had said or done...
No, don't explain. GOD BLESS US EVERY ONE!
I, too, am very pious, most devout:
I cross myself... twelve times (or thereabout)
Before I take my morning tea each day!
At lunch I'm up to forty, and I'd say
By night fall it's...a staggering amount,
But what a foolish waste of time to count!
DEVOTION COMES TO NOTHING IF WE COME
TO SUMMARIZE DEVOTION IN A SUM.
A tiny play on words...doth please you not?
I swear I made it up right on the spot!
I don't know how I do it, I just... do.
These epigrams, they...come to me as dew
Collects upon a budding daffodil.
A curse? A blessing? Call it what you will,
It's mine to bear this "genius of the word"
DID I SAY "GENIUS"? I think it's absurd
When people call you that, don't you agree?
To us it comes like breath so naturally
It seems like sorcery to those below!
I cite that telling phrase from Cicero:
"DE BONUM EST"..."DIS BONUM EST"...O, shit...
Well, anyway, you get the gist of it.
I do love Latin. Does it show? It's true!
I'm something of a scholar in it, too.
I've read them all (yes, even I'm impressed)
From Cicero to... you know...all the rest...
Whom I could quote in full without abatement.
But I digress.

ELOMIRE

    O, what an understatement.

VALERE

That meal! You must have gone to great expense!
How cruel of me to keep you in suspense!
DID I enjoy it? WAS the meal a hit?
I've turned you slowly, slowly on the spit.
Be at your ease, my friends! I thought the meal
Was excellent... if not...you know... "ideal."
The vinaigrette: a touch acidic, no?
And I prefer less runny haricots,
More butter in the veloute next time,
And who, for heaven's sake, told you that lime
Could substitute for lemon in souffle...?
These tiny points aside, please let me pay
My compliments to all your company,
So generous in breaking bread with me
(Albeit bread that was a wee bit stale),
But I don't want to nitpick. Did I fail
To mention what a charming group they are?
Marquise-Therese! She's going to be a star!
A huge one! And it's not because she sings
Her talent is for... Much bigger things
As for the others, well they tend to be
A little too... "theatrical" for me
But, darling, otherwise, words can't describe
My deep affection for your little tribe
With whom, I do amuse myself to think,
I shall be privileged to eat and drink
(As we have done this evening) every night!
That is, of course, assuming it's all right
Am I mistaken? Stop me if I am.
But it seemed obvious to this old ham
That we had an immediate rapport.
Well-educated people I adore!
It's such a joy to know there's no confusion
When I, whose speech is peppered with allusion,
Refer to facts which few but scholars know
Arcane, pedantic things like... Cicero
And...other famed oddments of that kind
(Which, to the truly cultivated mind,
Are common knowledge more than erudition...)
But I digress! O, damn me to perdition!
"SHUT UP! SHUT UP! GIVE SOMEONE ELSE A CHANCE!"
I've had that said to me all over France.
All over Europe, if the truth be told
To babble on completely uncontrolled
Is such a dreadful, dreadful, DREADFUL vice!
Me, I keep my sentences concise
And to the point... (well, nine times out of ten)
Yes, humanly, I falter now and then
And when I do, naive enthusiasm
Incites a sort of logorrheic spasm
A flood! I mean I don't come up for air!
And even though such episodes are rare
I babble on... you can't imagine how
(My God! I'm almost doing it right now!)
NO, NO! I'M ONLY JOKING! NOT TO FEAR!

In fact, I'm far more guilty, so I hear,
Of smugly showing that "My lips are sealed...
When I'm the leading expert in the field!
Of haughtily refusing to debate
When I could easily pontificate!
Instead, I turn away with icy mien
And look...intimidating serene:
As if... you know... the wisdom of the ages
Were silently inscribed upon the pages
Of some majestic tablet in my mind.
But I lay claim to nothing of the kind!
It's others who surround me with this lore,
Myself, I know I'm just a troubadour
With very few accomplishments to boast...
But, then, I'm more self-critical than most.
You think me too self-critical?! Alack,
Ten thousand more have launched the same attack!
That's awfully good: "...have launched the same attack!"
"Ten thousand more have launched the same attack!"
"YOU THINK ME TOO SELF-CRITICAL"?! ALACK,
TEN THOUSAND MORE HAVE LAUNCHED THE SAME ATTACK!
That's VERY close to genius, don't you think?
It only... YES! You HAVE a quill and ink!
I would be very grateful... may I please?
No time to lose when lightning strikes the trees!
What did I say again? How did it go?
(Keep talking...I'm listening, you know:
This won't take me a second.) Yes, that's right!
"Ten thousand more..." O, what a pure delight!
One must act quickly on one's inspirations
That they're preserved for future generations;
Behaving otherwise, it seems to me,
Ignores the grave responsibility
Imposed on us (for it's not ours to choose)
By...what?..."the lyric gift"..."the tragic muse"...
I translate rudely from the words in Greek,
But any tongue sounds coarse when used to speak
Of something so ineffable and high
Believe me, greater scriveners than I.
(All right, not "greater", "different": is that fair?)
Have racked their brains and torn out all their hair
In vain pursuit of some linguistic sign
To name the art of uterus divine
But what? Poetizing that's too crude
And I'm a stickler for exactitude
Who chafes at clumsy, earthbound turns of phrase
True eloquence rings out like godly praise:
There's no mistaking it, it just takes wing
And, frankly, my own word, "createring"
Seems loftiest... more lofty than the Greek!
O! HOW DISGRACEFUL! SLAP ME ON THE CHEEK!
WHAT HUBRIS! WHAT VULGARITY! WHAT NERVE!
NO, SLAP ME! SLAP ME! THAT'S WHAT I DESERVE!
What gall that I, the commonest of sods,
Presume to speak more finely that the gods!
Of course it may be true, that's not the point!
What's ugly is my choosing to anoint
Myself instead of giving you the chance.
No doubt you both must look at me askance
For such a gross, conceited indiscretion:
I pray it won't affect your good impression.
I'm so relieved to get that off my chest!
Now that we've put that nagging point to rest
I shall return to my initial theme,
Which is, in short, in fact, to wit, I deem
By way of introduction, SILENCE ALL:
I HAVEN'T GOT A CLUE! BLANK AS A WALL!
NO, REALLY, I'M QUITE SENILE! IT'S NO JOKE!
MY HEAD IS LIKE AN EGG WITHOUT A YOLK!
AND DON'T THINK THIS IS JUST A WAY OF STALLING
MY MIND HAS BUCKLED... ISN'T THAT APPALLING!?
THERE'S NOTHING BUT A SPACE BETWEEN MY EARS!
One time I had amnesia in Algiers,
Where everyone is black who isn't white!
(But that's another tale... some other night.)
Suffice to say I lost a whole December...
Or was it August?...Whoops, I don't remember!
You see how absent-minded I can get!?
"WHEN DID YOU HAVE AMNESIA?" "I FORGET!"
Is that not comic genius? I must use it!
I'd better write it down before I lose it!
What did I say... again... about forgetting...?
O CHRIST! I've just FORGOTTEN! How UPSETTING!
COME BACK! COME BACK, YOU TANTALIZING GEM!
YOU TEASE! YOU BITCH! YOU FICKLE APOTHEGM!
I GAVE YOU LIFE, AND NOW YOU FLY FROM ME!!
This happens with annoying frequency
It leads me to exclaim and caterwaul!
Well! Now you've really seen me, warts and all
ALGERIAN AMNESIA! no, that's wrong,
O, never mind. More gems will come along,
They always do. Now where was I?... Ah, yes
You've seen me in a state of stark undress.
My warts exposed, my manner slightly odd
Well, what would you prefer? Some cheap façade

Of blemishless perfection? Not from ME!
GO ELSEWHERE, YE WHO SEEK DISHONESTY,
MY LIFE IS TRUTH, AND TRUTH MY GREATEST PASSION!
Good heavens, both of you are looking...ashen!
I've been too honest, haven't I? But when?
WHY CAN'T I LEARN RESTRAINT LIKE OTHER MEN
INSTEAD OF SPILLING EVEYTHING AT ONCE?
THE VINAIGRETTE! OF COURSE! I'M SUCH A DUNCE!
HOW COULD I? Please accept my deep regret!
Look, I...enjoy...acidic...vinaigrette....
It really makes me...PUKE!!!...O!!! THERE, YOU SEE!
I CANNOT LIE! DAMN MY INTEGRITY!
I want to spare your feelings, yes, I do,
But that means saying things that aren't true,
And of my meager talents, that's not one.
You see, I find that dwelling in the sun
Of honest criticism brings more joy
Than rotting in the darkness of some coy
And sycophantic coterie of slaves.
God! Eloquence comes over me in waves!
Did you hear that one? We all raised our brows...
Permit me...just the... tiniest of bows,
I thank you very much, you're far too kind;
As Cicero has famously opined,
"To hear one's peers applaud," ...no! that's not it!
You know the one...the famous one...O, shit!
THE...ONE ABOUT...THE NOBLEMEN...COMPETING...
Well, it's so famous it's not worth repeating.
The point is, when a man whom I revere

As highly as the famous ELOMIRE
Should greet my stabs at wit with such approval,
I faint...go fetch a cart for my removal!
It's true. No, absolutely, I'm not acting:
The lights grow dim, my pupils are contracting,
My knees go wobbly and my knuckles white,
I'm fading out. Goodnight, sweet world, goodnight...
I'm totally unconscious now, I swear.
CAN ANYBODY HEAR ME? ARE YOU THERE?
Perhaps you think I'm being too dramatic;
But, really, I just droop when I'm ecstatic.
What causes that? Do either of you know?
A mystic in Gibraltar said I'm low
In some peculiar energy which lies
(For Leos, Capricorns, and Geminis)
Astride the cusp of Saturn's largest moon.
Well, fine. But does that tell me why I swoon?
Of course it doesn't! What a lot of bunk!
Believe in that stuff and you're really sunk!
Thank God our age has banished superstitions!
(Except for things like sprites and premonitions
Which I think almost certainly are true;
And voodoo dolls and fetishism, too.
Seem eminently credible to me
And tarot cards and numerology
And cabalistic rituals and such....)
But that astrology! Now there's a crutch
That's used by fools with half a brain, or none...
WELL, SPEAK OF VISIONS! SOFT! I'M HAVING ONE!

Opening Night – Octobe

O

ing in a public square in Ghent
Ghent. It look looks like Ghent.
say it's Ghent.") …It's Ghent.)
nner reads: "A Great Event:
ALERE and ELOMIRE Present
ant Spectacle Hailed All Through France…"
he title.) "ROMAN…," no, "ROMANCE
THING…SOMETHING…" Then "The Town of Ghent"
u it was Ghent.) Then there's a tent
ch throngs the very cream of Flanders!
rsion (though it almost panders
ng such glory to my dream
wo cloths sewn neatly at the seam
s might, someday, this world enfold.)
erely? Or a truth foretold?
eone say which of the two he thinks it?
r I answer, that would only prove it,
a cranky governess gone gray
hat phrase in Zürich, by the way,
s EIGHT YEARS OLD! YES, ONLY EIGHT!
? Try PHENOMENAL! Try GREAT!
provoked just knew not ends.
ow despised I was by friends!
ell in love with me of course;
"my every word a tour-de-force!
for doting on me so,
I was a…strapping lad, you know…
at me as if I led him on!
ne a child before you'd blame a don!!??

I ONLY DID WHAT I WAS TOLD TO DO!!
LIES! I NEVER JUMPED HIM! THAT'S NOT TRUE!
Good heavens! Suddenly it all came back!
So sorry…seems I wandered off the track…)
Um…FATE!…that's right…a governess gone gray.
She guides our every movement, and I'd say
Her stewardship goes well beyond the grave.
But if all things are fated, why be brave…?
Or noble? Or industrious? Or fair?
Is that all you can do? Just blankly stare?
Don't tell me this has never crossed your mind!
If not, you've waltzed through life completely blind!
Such questions are essential, don't you see?
A solid grounding in philosophy
Is vital to a proper education!
It never entered my imagination
That you could tack this bare necessity…
(The things I just assume! Well, foolish me!)
At risk of sounding pompous or uncouth,
I'd like to list some volumes from my youth
Which might flesh out the…bald spots in your learning.
They've made my brain more subtle and discerning,
Those great Moroccan-bound and gold-tooled classics,
Which we the prefects in our flowing cassocks
Had tucked beneath our arms…I smell them, still!
Indulge me for a moment, if you will
I recommend you read…no, I insist…
An author whom, remarkably, you've missed
Since he's the cornerstone of ancient thought
(And if he's not already should be taught
To every child in every French lycée.)
His name, of course, is…wait, it starts with "A"…
A very famous name, don't help me out;
I know it's "A"; it's "A" without a doubt.
It starts with "A." It's "A." Or maybe "D."
No, "A." It's "A." I'm sure it's "A." Or "P."
I could be "P." Or "M." It's "M." IT'S "M."!!
O, never mind. It could be all of them.
Well, this is terrible; I'm just appalled.
My God! He wrote the famous…WHAT'S-IT-CALLED.
COME ON! Don't leave me hanging on a limb!
You're acting like you've never heard of him,
And everybody has. He's world renowned!
His writings turned philosophy around
By altering the then-prevailing view
That what is real is really falsely true
To what is true is really falsely real.
Well, either way, it's BRILLIANT! Don't you feel?
And I'm not saying I don't see the holes;
Still, it's a stunning glimpse into our souls
No matter how you slice it, Q.E.D.
(He won a prize for it…deservedly.)
But who remembers prizes? It's the FAME!
The names of brilliant men like…what's-his-name…
Can never be forgotten: that's the PRIZE!
Such men live on when everybody dies!
They laugh at famine, pestilence and drought:
And isn't that what life is all about?
In any case, we've really talked a-streak!
Aren't you exhausted? Me? I'm feeling WEAK!!
We've hardly met, and yet you're like my brother
The way we banter and play off each other.
We've chatted, chortled, changed our points of view,
We've laughed a little, cried a little, too.
We've had some hills, some valleys and plateaus,
We've traded secrets, quipped in cryptic prose.
We've dropped our guards, we've learned to give a damn!
We've proudly cried, "Yes! This is who I am!"
We've said it all, and then…found more to say,
In short, we've…quote, "just talked the night away."
And surely that's a sign, at least to me,
That this our partnership was meant to be!
For though we're strangers (in a narrow sense),
In several ways more striking and intense
Our gift for words, our love of the sublime
We've known each other since the dawn of time!
O, very pretty "…since the dawn of time!"
"WE'VE KNOWN EACH OTHER SINCE THE DAWN OF TIME!"
Well, good! That's all I really planned to say,
Except to thank you for a fine soiree
Spoiled only by acidic vinaigrette,
But then I've said that…more than once, I'll bet!
My head is in the clouds: pay no attention!
It's off in some ethereal dimension
Where worldly thoughts not instantly deleted
Are roundly and mechanically repeated
As if engaging the earth below.
How galling it must be for you to know
That even as we speak, within my mind
I might be off in some place more refined
That even though I'm present by convention,
You may not really have my full attention!
I don't mean you specifically, dear friend!
Good heavens! Would I dare to condescend
To someone as illustrious as you!?

I mean, of course, the common people who
Would stoop to kiss my hem they so adore me:
Forgive them, Lord! They know not how they bore me
With idle chatter of their simple ways!
I'm sorry, but my eyes begin to glaze
And it's a chore to keep myself from snoring
When someone's jawing on about their boring crop concerns
Oh no a blighted grape (my kids are all going to die)
I smile and nod, but silently escape
To knowledgeable regions in my dome
More crowded than a Roman hippodrome!
I have, for instance (and it's not a fluke)
Verbatim recall of the Pentateuch!
Incredible? It's true! Attend and see:
From Genesis to Deuteronomy
I now recite the Scriptures, LEARNED BY HEART!!:
"IN THE BEGINNING…"…yes, well that's the start;
It goes on just like that till Moses dies.
A superhuman task to memorize?
Not really. It's so good, it rather stuck…
But I digress! SHUT UP YOU STUPID CLUCK,
AND LET THESE GENTLE PEOPLE TALK A MITE!
Look, gag me with this handkerchief, all right?
I know that sounds extreme, and I'm a stranger,
But trust me: you are in the gravest danger!
For my digressions (left unchecked) can reach
The vast proportions of a major speech;
And you have no idea how close I am
To just that sort of frantic dithyramb!
So why not spare yourselves a living hell
And gag me! GAG ME! TIE ME UP, AS WELL!
RESTRAIN ME! DISCIPLINE ME! HOLD ME BACK!
HUMILIATE ME! GIVE THE WHIP A CRACK
DISGRACE ME: MAKE ME BARK AND WEAR A DRESS
AND LICK THE FILTHY FLOOR CLEAN UP THIS MESS
Rub my nostrils in your filthy socks
And if you have to lock me in this box
But in the meantime, gagged I should remain.
It's better that way, no? It's such a sane
And healthy way to curb my domination.
I find it a complete abomination
(No matter how distinguished one might be)
When every word is "ME ME ME ME ME,"
ME, I'm far too interested in others.
And frankly, friends, were I to have my "druthers"
I'd utter not a peep for weeks untold,
Preferring to…absorb the manifold
Of human speech: the "babel" of the masses.
Just stop and listen to the lower classes!
You'll have an education when you're done
That rivals twenty years at the Sorbonne!
For in their mindless grunts, the bourgeoisie
Express what I call "wise stupidity."
But not one listens anymore, I fear,
And when I die, so too will disappear
That subtle art, whose practice now grows faint.
And I'm not saying I'm some stained-glass saint
Who always listens. Always? No, indeed!
My God! I'm human! Cut me and I bleed!
It's simply that, as far as mortals go,
I'm sensitive (and some say too much so)
To any nuance in a conversation
Which might, PERHAPS, suggest my domination.
Thus, in mid-sentence often I just cease…
(Despite the countless times I've held my peace
When, in the end, I might as well have chattered
Since only I said anything that mattered!
I know that sounds repulsive, but it's true.)
The point is, this is something that I do
Against all logic; so don't be distraught
If, in the middle of a brilliant thought,
I stop like this…depriving you of more;
Or if, commanding reverence from the floor
For awesome skills debating pro or con,
I simply stop like.this…and don't go on!
A trifle strange, n'est-ce pas? But, if you please,
Ask any of my many devotees:
They'll tell you that this quirk (at first appearing)
In time becomes…incredibly endearing!
To me it seems obnoxious, heaven knows,
But most say it's a charming trait that grows
More sweet with each encounter! TELL ME WHY!
I just don't see it…but, then who am I?
At any rate, THE GAG! OF COURSE! Let me,
Observe with what profound simplicity
It does the job. I think you'll be surprised.
VOILA! Now isn't this more civilized!
I'm silenced and I think we're all relieved!
We've nipped me in the bud, and thus retrieved
The limelight for our precious Elomire.
Speak on, my friend! This player longs to hear
It in posterity you'll deign to share
Your splendid name with on AUGUSTE VALERE!
Please answer lest I talk you both to death
I wait on your reply with bated breath.

Sometimes you are lucky enough to see genius at work in real life. Every time Mark Rylance soared through this colossal monologue you knew you were in the presence of someone truly great. During rehearsals I had to put hankies in my mouth to prevent myself from sobbing with laughter. Golden days: as gold as the fusillade of gold confetti that heralded the princess's entrance.

177

Being Fabulous

Right: Eddy and Patsy hit Paris. Pats believes she is looking fabulous.

Below: looking pretty fab before the day has really started; smoking de rigeur.

This is how it happened. Ruby Wax had come to see *Vanilla*, our doomed play on Shaftesbury Avenue, and she came backstage where we met for the first time. She said I should be working with Dawn French and Jennifer Saunders, but would I appear in her own show before that. I loved working with Ruby as she was completely anarchic, and preferred to improvise; and so we made up what we would do and say.

A few months later a script arrived out of the blue and I thought: I have never seen anything like this before, or laughed so much at a piece of writing. It was the pilot for a show to be called *Absolutely Fabulous* and Jennifer Saunders was the writer. I remember meeting her for the first time and she seemed intimidatingly opaque. I read through a scene with her and the producer Jon Plowman but I couldn't seem to make my character Patsy sound like the person she was hoping for. Jennifer can be very silent; on this occasion I felt so inadequate that I went back home, rang my agent and said: 'Get me out of this.'

'Oh come on,' she said, 'It's only a pilot, it may never get made, and anyway you are skint.'

All I can remember is inventing (for myself) a person, largely based on a cartoon version of me, who had her own life and history, and a way of walking with a hunched back, and a sneery voice, and trying it out in scenes with Jennifer. Once I got her to laugh I went on with more of the same. Patsy seemed to spring fully-formed into the world, with her heavy smoking and alley-cat morals, her sponging attitudes and foul language, and her undying jealousy of Saffy. Jennifer had opened a Pandora's box for me with her outrageously inventive writing. I don't know how or where she got her ideas from, but they were all new and fresh, shocking and desperately funny. She cast June Whitfield as her mother and Julia Sawalha as her daughter; Bubble

was originally to be a Sloane Ranger but as soon as Jennifer met Jane Horrocks she wanted Jane's accent.

With the confidence of genius, Jennifer would allow us to bring our own ideas about how our characters might develop; rehearsing for those shows was easily one of the happiest times of my life because we just laughed till we cried, day after day, suddenly sobering up for the live performances in front of an audience at BBC Television Centre. Every Friday, when the great theme tune 'Wheels on Fire', re-recorded by Ade Edmondson and Julie Driscoll, blared out into the darkened studio our hearts thudded and we would stare at each other, mouthing our lines or trying out a piece of business that had to work to get a laugh. It felt like a smash hit from the very first show: in the audience were not only Dawn French and Lenny Henry, but Ade, Ben Elton, Ruby Wax and a tooth-loosening bunch of top comedians which rather focussed the mind. But the applause and the gales of laughter told us all we needed to know: this one was going to run. But how far?

Of course we hoped it would be familiar to Londoners, and maybe the South-West of the country... but what about people who hadn't heard of Harvey Nicks and had no knowledge of the PR industry? The truth is that if a comedy is well written it doesn't matter where it is set or even who is in it. If it works, it works worldwide.

We filmed extracts in the South of France and Morocco, New York and Paris, always returning to record the complete show in front of a live audience; they can tell if something is funny, and we often had to hold up the filming until the hysteria subsided. It didn't seem to matter if we forgot lines, or if gags went wrong: the audience just howled for more. Edina's appalling taste in expensive clothes, and her exotic yet slutty lifestyle, struck a chord with them. For the first time on television a family was shown to be truly dysfunctional, with naked greed and bullying on show, and people laughed and called for more.

Patsy, who like me had been a model in the sixties, progressed from being a bitch to a witch, with many of her internal organs removed due to her catastrophic addictions to sex and drugs and rock'n'roll. Bubble was an airhead without any perceptible cognitive skills or abilities: Mother was light-fingered and blithely outspoken, Saffy was...well, Saffy was the only normal one in the show, a role which Julia mysteriously made completely unforgettable and sympathetic without a trace of goody-goodyness. Bob Spiers directed most of the early shows, and the comedy was served perfectly by his cool eye for humour and his ability to let the writing carry the show. We flew by Concorde to New York and back in a day, just to photograph a door-handle. We went on a photo-shoot to Morocco and Patsy sold Saffy in the souk. We rented a chateau in France but were too vain and silly

Jennifer often forges my signature and I hers: this is a rare item where we both appeared to have signed our own names. She can imitate my voice as well. We had both just finished a third margarita.

EDINA & PATSY CONTINUE THEIR OUTRAGEOUS ANTICS
IN THE AWARD-WINNING COMEDY

ABSOLUTELY FABULOUS

Starring: Jennifer Saunders, Joanna Lumley,
Julia Sawalha, June Whitfield & Jane Horrocks

BBC *TELEVISION*

Outside Edina's house. The inside was always a set in the studios. Edina had it re-decorated several times during the run of the show.

to find out where, as we were afraid of speaking French and ended up in a damp hut playing ping-pong. We were carted downstream unconscious on a rubbish barge, and got married by Whoopi Goldberg in New York in a gay ceremony, simply through Edina trying to track down her son Serge, who had long fled his home to escape her stifling presence. People sometimes quote lines from the show to me and I may not remember them; but I only have to say 'Cheers, sweetie' for Patsy to come lurching out of my mouth, like a vampire from a darkened cellar.

I don't know to this day how many programmes or series we made. I do remember that after Series Three we stopped for FIVE YEARS: the show was by now a huge smash in America, and indeed all round the world, but Jennifer, inscrutable as the Sphinx, simply didn't feel like

PRESS SERVICE

BBC PRESS OFFICE   TELEVISION CENTRE, WOOD LANE, LONDON W12 7RJ. TELEPHONE: 081-576 1865

ABSOLUTELY FABULOUS

EDINA AND PATSY ARE BACK!

Those fashion victims from hell, Edina and best-friend Patsy, otherwise known as Jennifer Saunders and Joanna Lumley are back in the eagerly awaited second series of the award-laden 'Absolutely Fabulous' on Thursday, January 27 on BBC-1.

Edina's daughter Saffron (Julia Sawalha), her abstracted Mother (June Whitfield), and assistant Bubbles (Jane Horrocks) manage to lead near normal lives, despite Edina's histrionic battles against what she sees as the unfair forces of nature and society ranged against her.

Edina and best-friend Patsy continue to tread on life's toes as they single-mindedly set about gratifying their lusts - be it fashion, food or fad.

Just some of the slings and arrows of fate Edina encounters in the new series, are having to find a new best friend after a row with Patsy, intimations of mortality after a death in the family, a sudden drop in income and living standards, re-birthing and an overseas business trip.

In the first episode Patsy finds herself embroiled in a front-page tabloid sex scandal, and Edina who demands medical attention at the best hospital for a minor complaint, discovers that you don't always get what you pay for.

Guest stars in the series include Mandy Rice-Davis, Lulu, Britt Ekland, Zandra Rhodes, Helena Bonham-Carter, Germaine Greer, Susi Quatro, Helen Lederer, Kathy Burke, Richard E Grant, Lady Penelope, Patrick Barlow, John Wells and Mark Wing-Davey.

'Absolutely Fabulous' is written by Jennifer Saunders, directed by Bob Spiers and produced by Jon Plowman.

FURTHER INFORMATION:

ROSENBERG

Us with Zandra Rhodes, Lulu and Britt Ekland, whom Patsy admired and with whom she tried unsuccessfully to form a friendship. From the press release the guest stars shine with a dazzling magnetism.

Episode one, where I found that Patsy was never able to be photographed without lapsing into tired old modelling poses. Mother's hair is brown, as we are only in our late teens. Mrs Monsoon was kind to 'Old Patsy', having her over for tea and remaining unfazed by her unpleasant attitude.

In Marilyn Manson mode Abfab

Patsy dressed for a Marilyn Manson concert with exceptional care, even going so far as to wearing a specially made contact lens.

When Edina had a shotgun wedding to her first husband, played by Chris Malcolm, Patsy turned up unsuitably dressed in hot pants, while Eddy sullenly tries to cover her bump with the bouquet.

writing any more at the time. This attitude was unheard of in the States, where if a show is a hit you buckle down to working on it, year after year, for at least thirty-six episodes a year. And here we were, doing six a year and then stopping altogether. Of course we came back; and of course we shall come back again, as she has created something which has got into the bloodstream of the nation and defies time. It doesn't matter how old we are: we have filmed flash-forward sequences, in which Edina and Patsy are well into their eighties, still smoking and drinking and behaving appallingly. I love playing very old Patsy, in prosthetic make-up with balding head and loose false teeth. I feel that when I let things go I shall look exactly like that. Being papped (photographed by paparazzi) holds no fear for me, as it is almost impossible to look more disgusting than I do as old Patsy (or old Delilah Stagg in 'Jam and Jerusalem' which Jennifer wrote as well. She sees me as a very repellent old creature: I wonder why this is).

Our clothes were extremely important. Edina simply got the newest and most outrageous fashion garments and dragged her plump body into them (Jennifer often wore a fat suit underneath); whether or not they fitted her, or were in any way attractive, was immaterial to her

A fabulous moment: Patsy, supposedly burnt to a crisp in the fire she started by falling asleep with a lighted cigarette between her lips, rises like some ghastly phoenix from the wreckage of Eddy's kitchen. While the audience was distracted by something at the other side of the set, I crept in laid my head on the table and was covered with soot. There was a yell of surprise when the thing lifted its head and was Patsy, quite undamaged and still smoking.

187

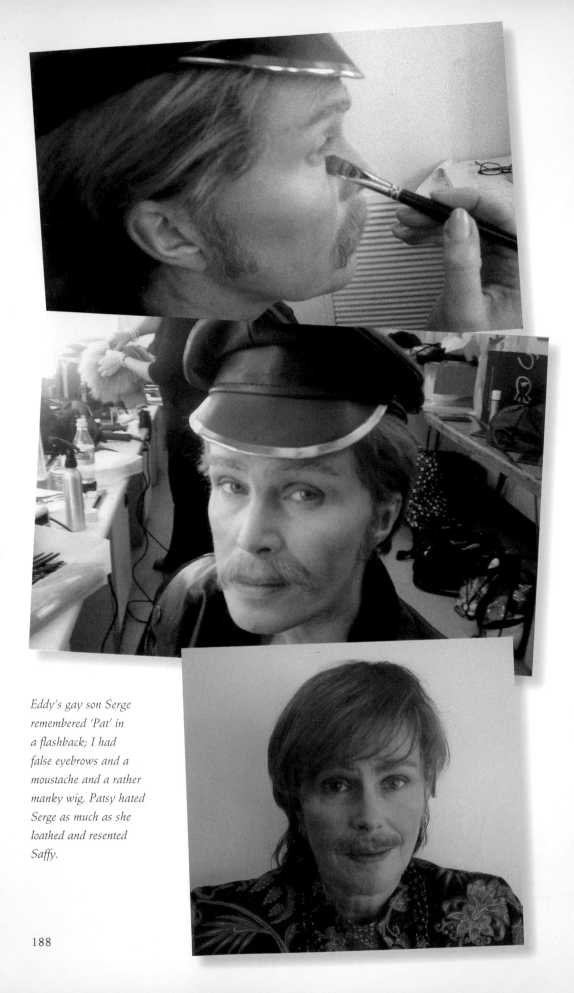

Eddy's gay son Serge remembered 'Pat' in a flashback; I had false eyebrows and a moustache and a rather manky wig. Patsy hated Serge as much as she loathed and resented Saffy.

vanity. Patsy always started the day looking good, dressed by Betty Jackson mainly, but also Bruce Oldfield, Chanel and Jasper Conran. By the time evening came, and many beverages had been taken, she was liable to unravel into a tramp with smeared lipstick and straggly hair. Her beehive grew higher and higher. It was all my own hair, backcombed to a frenzy and sprayed within an inch of its life. Jennifer called it Mr Whippy. We discovered that Pats had once decided to be a man, and had gone to Morocco to have an operation, in the distant past when the Beatles released the Sergeant Pepper album: but whatever she had had stitched on, withered away and disappeared, so she shaved off her moustache and reverted to being a man-eating ashtray.

Eddy and Patsy in Morocco, with John Wells playing a very suspect 'uncle'. This was when Patsy's operation to become a man seemed to have been a success. Much dope smoked, as seen in John's face. Edina and Patsy slavishly influenced by the Beatles at this stage. Mocked-up newspaper headlines and magazine covers are all part and parcel of film making.

In Val D'Isere, where Patsy couldn't get off the ski lift and went round and round all night.

Outside the florist Moyses Stevens in Sloane Street: something about Eddy trying to find a suitable donation for the begging man and Patsy outraged that she is going to give away lovely miniatures of good spirits.

Patsy keeps her head on top of the 67th floor of a Manhattan skyscraper. Behind and below is Central Park. I have vertigo, and Jennifer, arriving by helicopter to rescue her friend from the tedium of office life, can't stand flying. All in all, a brave day.

Patsy's false memory kicks in; she believes she really is as good as Erin O'Connor and imagines a photo-shoot where she and the supermodel were buddies. I love this picture, as pathetic as it may seem; for a second I feel I, Joanna, WAS there, WAS for a fleeting moment up there with today's greats of modelling. Not much retouching needed. Fab.

192

Not surprisingly, the gay community thought the world of the show and of Edina and Patsy in particular. Their outrageous appearance and easily-copied behaviour made them perfect subjects for a mass of imitations on Gay Pride marches and Mardi Gras floats. Champagne was more readily referred to as 'Bolly' after the show came out, Edina's expensive taste for once making the right selection.

When I was dressed as Patsy there was nothing I couldn't say or do. I became her, spoke her vile language without thinking twice, behaved hatefully to Saffy without a care in the world. She was so much the opposite of me and yet...and yet. Deep down inside I recognise her, and her own hopelessly abusive upbringing, and her utter dependence on the only friend she had in the world, Edina Monsoon. We haven't finished with them yet; there are more stories to be told and much more chaos to be wrought. I hear Jennifer's voice calling, and my hand reaches for the mirror: let the backcombing begin.

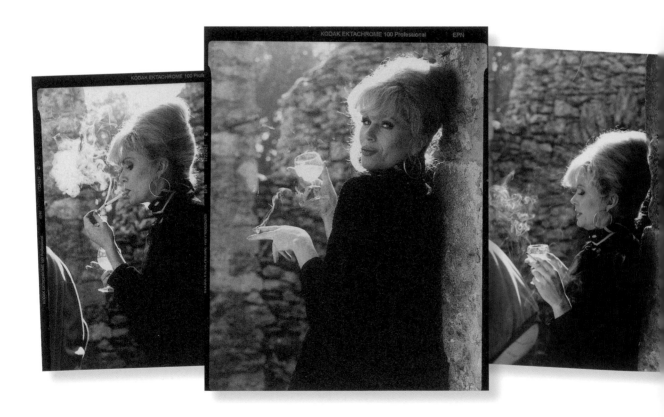

Jennifer can do anything she sets her mind to: here she snaps Patsy lighting up in the doorway of their French hovel, and opposite, slightly the worse for wear, after a successful wine-tasting. On location we have big coats from wardrobe to keep us warm, as the days are long and the weather is often cold and damp (see contents page).

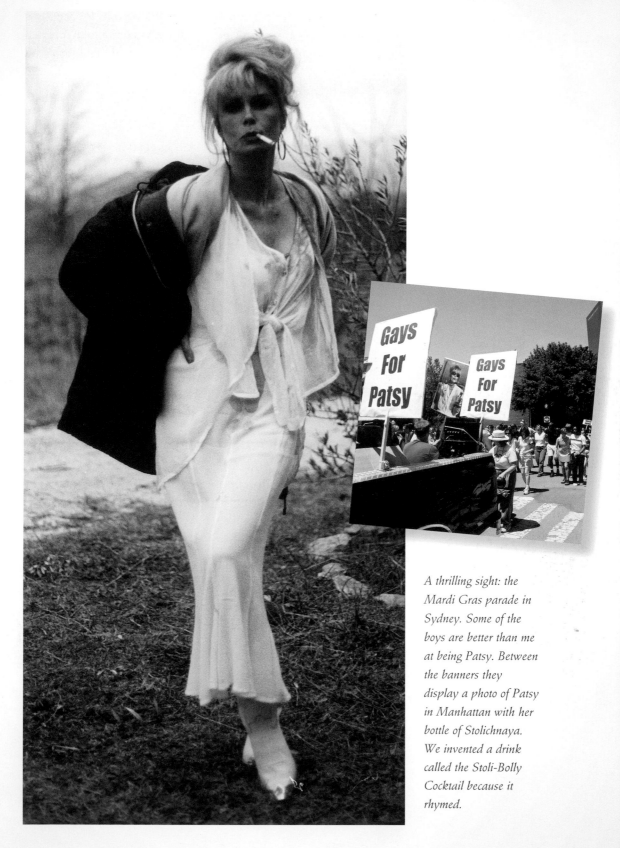

A thrilling sight: the Mardi Gras parade in Sydney. Some of the boys are better than me at being Patsy. Between the banners they display a photo of Patsy in Manhattan with her bottle of Stolichnaya. We invented a drink called the Stoli-Bolly Cocktail because it rhymed.

195

On the left a montage made by Jennifer for me, and below, one made by a fan.

Rehearsal room at Acton, since sold and redeveloped. The sets were marked out
on the floor in tape, the principal sets being Eddy's bedroom, the kitchen and the
living room. The top picture shows the way the bones of the kitchen are marked
out so that we can be sure that what we practise here will work in the studio.
Once the script was finalised we didn't add anything or the cameras wouldn't be
prepared. It's a skill to sound as though you are improvising.

Left: being lippy with Sarah Burns, costume mistress for many of the shows. She chose what we wore: often the clothes were on loan and had to be returned.

Below: I still have the red Donna Karan top seen here with a diamante buckled belt. Eddy was going through a Sex And the City phase and is looking very chic – for her. Comedy Central was the first to broadcast Ab Fab in the States, securing for them our eternal devotion.

Overleaf: authentic Ab Fab greeting cards. Others were made without permission which spoke when opened. Only then did I realize what people thought we sounded like.

As Good as it Gets

As one's face becomes more and more familiar a hundred exciting invitations arrive every week. There is nothing nicer than giving prizes and cutting ribbons; charities and businesses depend on publicity, and it is good sense to choose someone who will attract the press along to cover an event; if you are on television at the time you are more likely to get attention for the cause. Sometimes you must make a speech, say a few words about the railway, or supermarket, or charity gala. I always ask for a full briefing of the organisation beforehand so that you can talk facts and figures if necessary: but mostly people just want you to be there to endorse their cause and enjoy their hospitality, and be in their photographs.

So many thousands of wonderful charities exist in our country: I read that a new charity is formed every half hour in the United Kingdom. You can't support them all even if you want to: your day job is still there, and your family is still waiting to be fed and loved, but the idea that with such a small gesture you might be able to help raise money for a worthy cause is irresistible. I say yes to as many things as I possibly can because it is such good fun, and it is a fascinating way to get under the skin of the charity, or factory or ceremony, and to meet the generous and dedicated people behind them. When journalists ask whom I admire most, or which person has most influenced me, it is always the selfless charity workers behind the scenes who come top of my list. At home and at school I was taught that doing things for other people rather than for yourself is not only more important but more rewarding in the long run. It is true too; it is more exciting to give a present than to receive one, and strangely more thrilling to spend money on others than on yourself. The idea of pampering oneself comes pretty low on my list of lovely things to do. (If this sounds a bit goody-two-shoes I must correct that impression at once: one of the greatest joys in an actor's life

is opening an ominously formal-looking envelope only to find inside a huge and unexpected repeat fee, for some show you had long since forgotten: lovely unexpected money.) So I say: 'Do unto others as you would have them do unto you'…it works.

And of course, there are all the people you would never even dream of meeting, from rock stars and heart surgeons, boxers and MPs, dancers and movie stars…to the Queen. When Her Majesty comes into a room there is an instant feeling of Something Huge About To Happen; will she stop and talk, or notice our group at all. Is it rude to stare very, very hard so you don't forget a single thing about that moment: will you remember every single syllable she utters, and try not to talk too much or too loudly or get onto some long-winded story you hope will amuse her…and then she is there! And words are exchanged and she is tiny and beautiful…and then she has moved on, and we all stand round grinning like fools. It is nearly the same thing with the Dalai Lama and Nelson Mandela: I have seen the same effect when Muhammed Ali was in London, and noticed people almost fainting as President Clinton passed by, but at the top of the list for me is the Queen. (I think – I know – Elvis would have fitted into this category too.)

The next two pages have a crowd of famous faces at events throughout the years. In the first spread you will be able to pick out Twiggy, Robbie Williams behaving badly, author Jilly Cooper, the heart surgeon Dr Christian Barnard, Gordon Jackson, Daley Thompson (what a schmoozy hug), Sefton, the horse that survived the Hyde Park bombings with his keeper, Michael Aspel during his (and my time) at Capital Radio (I was a director of the station for eleven years): you can spot Brian Cant, and playwright Harold Pinter during the run of Vanilla *which he directed, Gordon Brown when he was Chancellor of the Exchequer (we were to meet again years later, at Number 10 Downing Street rather than Number 11), a lamb, an elephant, and my lovely Shire horse Madame Butterfly, with me dressed up to give you a clue as to her name.*

Turn the page, and in no particular order appear Ken Bruce and Sue Cook when we were presenting BBC's Children in Need, *John Travolta at the Baftas, Greta Scacchi, Frank Bruno who hates being photographed, Professor Anthony Clare (I had just been on his radio show), Prince Charles at Clarence House (I am reading out citations for an award on the stairs), Virginia McKenna with balloons at the naming of an aircraft: there is Terry Wogan (with the present Mrs Wogan), Lionel Blair, Ernie Wise at a barbeque, Terry Waite at the opening of the Emmaus centre in South Norwood, the great Bill Travers of the Born Free Foundation, Julian Lloyd Webber (promoting real ale or the 'Quiet Pint' or 'Pipe Down', with all my support), Penelope Keith, Darcey Bussell, Patricia Hodge and Her Majesty the Queen at the Royal Academy; and for good measure, Her Majesty again, with Sylvia Sims in the background, at the Imperial War Museum.*

The moment I love: "I now declare this arcade/building/ station/open!!!" and the snip of the scissors. I have cracked bottles of champagne which refused to smash and tried to cut tape with blunt blades; no-one seems to mind. Opening the Rolvenden Railway Station was a special honour as I had been brought up in the village.

205

The plaster cast is taken off my arm. I'm still brown from my time as Girl Friday on her desert island.

Behind me are the photographs they took to ensure that every possible view of me would be accurate. Steve Swales works on the clay model of my head. I decided to smile, so that if people wanted to pose with the waxwork she would look cheerful: and they could slip their arm through hers and become my new best friend.

Many years ago, Adel Rootstein had my head modelled for the mannequins used in shop window displays; once I spotted ten such figures in the window of a New York department store, but even though I stood in front of them on the sidewalk for twenty minutes no-one noticed that they were meant to be me. To be made as a waxwork for Madame Tussaud's twenty years later was a tremendous honour. I was measured from top to toe, from side to side, from collar-bone to shin and elbow to hip. My hands were cast, while I stood stock still until the plaster had hardened, but the head, after being measured from nostril to lip and forehead to chin, was sculpted freehand by Steve Swales. Eyeballs were brought along to check the colour of the iris against mine: a tray of teeth, like ivory piano keys, offered a matching enamel colour. Luckily I had just returned from being cast away on a desert island where I had got a bit thinner (from lack of any decent food in the nine days I was there) so my figure looked less pudgy than it might have done. What would I like to wear? Jean Muir, I decided and so Miss Muir supplied her own choice, a navy blue wool jacket

We look like twins, but her hair is a bit bigger, and somehow her eyes seem bluer, an easy mistake to make, as mine change colour all the time, from grey to blue to green to sludge.

and culottes, with solid silver buttons and a white silk jersey blouse.

The moment of unveiling seldom varies, apparently: it is always early in the morning, before Madame Tussaud's opens its doors to the public, so that there is a chance for the press photographs to make the next edition. Your model stands there, and you walk up to stand beside it: it is a strange emotion to be able to walk around yourself in real life, in 3D, as it were: is this how tall I am? Do I look like this from behind? My model has changed her clothes since Patsy came along: I think they felt that my clothes were too restrained, so a red dress was provided. The waxwork eventually moved from room to room, fitting into different scenarios, standing beside a piano or grinning with a group of comedians. Soon she will be gone, and her body will be melted down and her head removed to a shelf behind the scenes, where she will go on smiling, proud to be there, lucky to have been chosen, her long-lost hands for ever on her imaginary hips.

The near-to-nude shot, with the strange effect of skin-coloured hands contrasting with the grey clay of the model. Couldn't be happier. Or prouder.

From Here to Kingdom Come

*Opposite: Jamie in the
green shirt was the
youngest of the boys.
Our journey into the
high Karakorams was
punctuated by dances,
when the boys joined in,
and mud-slides when
we all got out to push
the vehicles. Asif Khan
gave me a Chinese
road-worker's hat made
of strong bamboo, rather
than plastic or metal.*

To Shimshal in the High Karakorams

I wasn't, but I feel as though I was born in a suitcase. Nothing sets the pulse racing as much as a map on the table and a case lying open on the floor; I love travelling, and feel it is in my bloodstream. The unknown attracts me like a magnet, and no matter how widely you travel the huge world is still rich in secrets and surprises. The chance to meet new people and eat different food, to find out about strange cultures and try to speak a difficult language…well, I cannot think of a greater thrill.

When Jamie was fourteen we were asked to join an expedition to a part of the world that my parents had known well: the North West Frontier, and the upper valleys of the Hunza region in Northern Pakistan. There were eleven of us, six young men who had just left school, Jamie and four adults. We set out to study the effects of the Ismaili religion on these remote regions, setting off from Rawalpindi and travelling through Abbottabad, where my sister had been born, to Gilgit and then on to Gulmit, a tiny village in the heart of the Karakoram mountain range. We travelled by jeep along the Karakoram Highway, sleeping in campsites, and leading a fairly rugged existence. There were landslips where the road disappeared altogether, and illnesses when everyone got sick from polluted water. The terrain was very rugged, scree and rock, with colossal gorges through which the grey Indus River rushed. Three of us, two boys and I, were joined by five Hunzakuts to make the arduous journey to Shimshal, a prison valley reached by a three-day journey through what seemed like the back of beyond. The scorching sun and strong winds, tiny stone huts and chilly glaciers made it wholly unforgettable. I wouldn't allow Jamie to come, as I didn't know for sure if we would make it there and back in safety. The bridges defied description, swinging perilously high above what looked like certain death. The village of

*The rough path to
Shimshal was exhaust-
ing. I got heat-stroke on
the first day.*

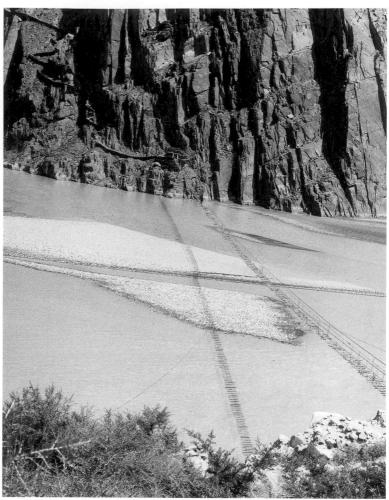

Try to imagine my fear at seeing this bridge for the first time. In the narrow gorges as we trudged eastwards towards Shimshal nothing moved but the wind, nothing sounded but the roar of the water below.

Shimshal was so hard to get to that it had been designated as a prison, as it was almost impossible to reach or escape from. Asif Khan, who led our expedition, was the younger brother of the great climber Shere Khan (like the tiger) who had accompanied Reinhold Messner on his mountaineering adventures.

The fellows from Hunza were tough and hugely good-humoured, moving like cats along paths that were only wide enough for a weasel. The tiny village, lying in a wide valley, had no roads as it had never seen a wheeled vehicle. The small dwellings had no chimneys, so smoke kippered you as you slept; but we were observed and welcomed with the greatest curiosity and kindness. The explorer Eric Shipton had written that the area was the most hostile he had ever crossed (which is quite something from the man who planned the successful ascent of Everest). No birds sang on the journey, and I only saw one flower in the seven days of our trek, a pale rose blooming by a boulder. In my daydreams I travel the route again; never before or since have I experienced such an extraordinary episode.

In Search of the White Rajahs

As a child in the Far East I had heard of the White Rajahs of Sarawak, an English family called Brooke, who had governed this small section of Borneo for a hundred years, running the tiny nation like a country estate. The film we made about their lives allowed us to travel as they would have done, paddling up rivers when there were no roads, sleeping in longhouses, trudging through jungles and trying to imagine how it was when head-hunters roamed the huge tracts of forest. The third and last Rajah, struggling to keep the country going after the Second World War, eventually sold Sarawak to the British government who in turn offered it to the newly-formed Federation of Malay States. The country changed hands for a million pounds.

Evidence still existed of the Rajahs' way of life; not grand but benevolent, with the Rajah making himself available to his people every evening at the Astana, the large bungalow that served as a 'palace'. I met and filmed his three daughters in America: they remembered rats in the roof, and no schooling, as they made their giddy way from Ascot to Sarawak's capital Kuching, from coming-out dances at the Ritz to the tropical downpours of an uncomfortable backwater jungle. Princess Gold, Princess Pearl and Princess Baba the press called them, although they weren't princesses; the middle sister, Elizabeth, married Harry Roy, the famous bandleader; he composed a song called 'Sarawakee' which was played in London nightclubs, while across the world the tribes of Sarawak, the Penan, Iban and Punan peoples had to get used to laying down their weapons against each other, as Rajah Brooke had outlawed head-hunting.

A safer bridge in Sarawak. The tropical climate brought back my upbringing in Malaya; hot and sweaty.

in S EARCH *of the* W HITE RAJAHS

A JOURNEY TO SARAWAK
WITH
JOANNA LUMLEY

BBC2

7.40 pm

Tuesday 24th September 1991
A WARNER SISTERS PRODUCTION

Learning to use a blow-pipe was easier than I thought;
I would never have wanted to kill a bird or animal but
target practice was fun.

217

The few days I spent in a longhouse were salutary. Grannies stayed behind to look after all the babies, the young and strong went into the jungle to get food and medicine from the trees, pigs and chickens rootled under the wooden huts built on stilts above the forest floor. The children went to school by canoe and were lively bright little people, silent and respectful the second an adult shushed them, leaping in and out of the river like glossy minnows, owning nothing, expecting nothing and somehow having everything. The men had their bodies tattooed in the most intricate patterns: running through dense foliage they were as invisible as jaguars. Once we witnessed a funeral wake, with villagers from far and wide arriving with presents for the deceased to take on her final journey: and she was buried upright, ready to walk off into the next world when the weeping and wailing had ceased. But the logging conglomerates were already bulldozing their way into their tribal way of life: and now the majestic rainforests have been felled to make garden furniture and disposable chopsticks, and the tribespeople have been rounded up and put in camps.

Opposite: In a long-house with the local chief, a charming courteous man who told me how much the tattoos hurt. He is dressed for dancing; the ancient costumes haven't changed through the ages.

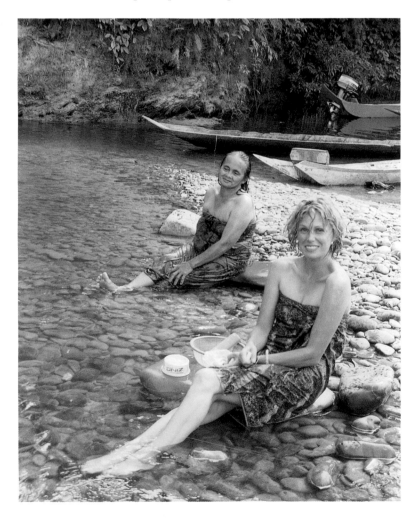

The boat woman and I washing our hair in the clear jungle stream. The water was as warm as a bath.

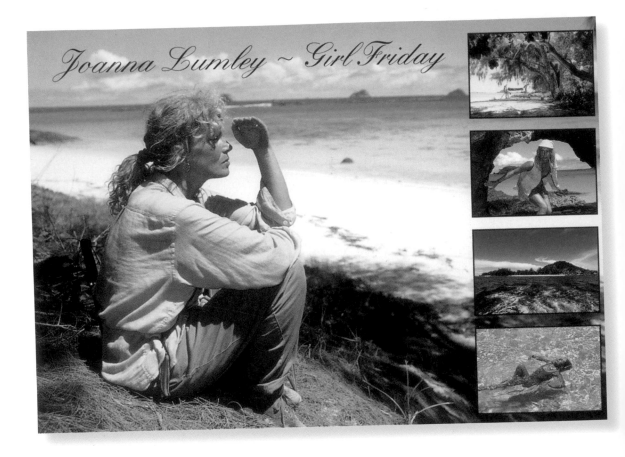

Joanna Lumley ~ Girl Friday

Girl Friday on the Island of Tsaranbanjina

Would Patsy be able to exist on a desert island without a supply of drink and with Harvey Nicks out of reach? We thought instead it would be more interesting to see if I, Joanna, could survive with barest minimum of help on a tiny island called Tsarabanjina, off the north west coast of Madagascar, for nine days. I would be Girl Friday; trained for what seemed like only twenty seconds by the Irish Guards in Pirbright (above right), I set off on my trip, utterly unprepared for the hardships ahead. For a start, I had only some knives and sacking, a torch, and a rusty tin to cook in: I was given only three teabags and a pound of rice, the clothes I stood up in and the SAS survival booklet to show me how to make a bed out of sticks. I was allowed my drawing pad and a pen, and a flint stone to make a spark to light a fire, but no hairbrush or soap, no toothbrush, or camera, or books to read. I had a survival tin given to me by the dear Micks, the Irish Guards, which had three matches, some string and needle and thread, but no binoculars, no dish or spoon, no music…how was I going to manage?

Opposite above: with the Micks at Pirbright, trying to absorb instructions on how to build an earth oven. Below: my humble allowance of necessary kit for island existence is spread out on the sacking. I am inspecting my three tea bags and rice ration.

useful
clothes
hooks

mosquito net

sacking

dodgy
lashing

Later I put
sticks across here
to make a shelf

The A-frame

Making the A-frame bed. By drawing things you remember them more clearly. The tall
poles had been left on the island by visiting fishermen but the place was deserted.

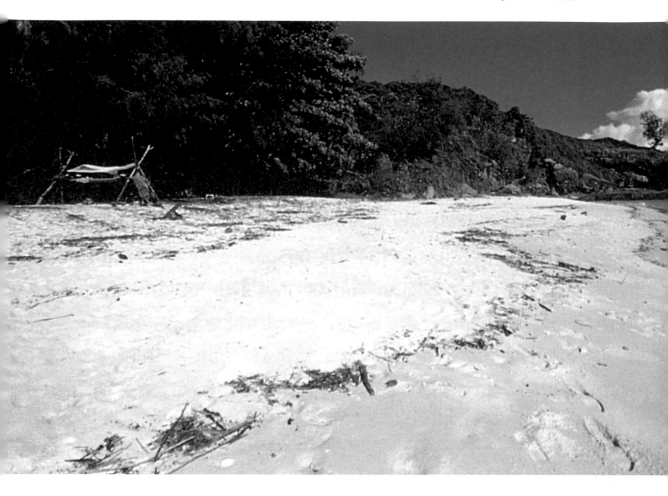

The small crew lived on a boat which was moored a mile out to sea: they came onto the island at first light, filmed all day and left before the sun set. A late monsoon meant that I had to live in a cave for four days, and when I returned to my bed, my A-frame bed that I had constructed laboriously on the beach when I arrived, it was full of twigs and insects. There was no fresh water supply, so I collected rainwater dripping off the rocks in a plastic bottle and purified it, which took ages. I found wood for the fire and spent hours carefully chopping the dry twigs into kindling and blowing on the embers to keep the flame alive for as long as it took to cook my grim supper each night, rusty rice with a fresh lime squeezed over to give it some taste, and eaten from a shell with a smaller shell serving as a spoon. The cave floor was sharp and rocky, cutting my bare feet, making my sodden-footed life miserable, so I cut up my cotton bra and stitched it to the insoles of my trainers to make the dearest little espadrilles.

The beach where I slept faced west. I watched the sunset, the flying foxes watched me.

The cave fire, with a tripod of twigs. The rusty can took ages to boil.

The cave fire

I watched turtle hatchlings trundling down to the waves: I was
entertained by a school of dolphins who leapt and dived for quarter of
an hour while I stood on the morning rocks above, shouting 'More!
More!' My head was full of music I remembered: songs and tunes
bubbled up, with poetry I had learned as a child: and, as hunger made
me dimmer, I became obsessed with collecting shells spreading them
out on the shelf of the A-frame bed. I propped one behind my candle
stub to lighten the darkness of the cave. I named parts of the island so
that I could remember where I was: Mosquito Alley, Skeleton Rock,
The Albert Hall.

For nine brief days, nine days of eternity, I owned the island, watched
over by flying foxes and fish eagles, surrounded by a crystal sea and the
call of sea birds. I drew a map from what I could see, putting in all the
coves and beaches. But I needn't have: it is securely sealed in my mind
for ever, as fresh now as when I left by helicopter in the baking heat
of my last afternoon, my footprints fading into the sand, a few shells
scattered by the shore, leaving no trace but the A-frame and a buried
offering of my rusty tin, a recipe for grubbed-up sweet potatoes and
my SAS survival book.

*My hair, caked with salt and sand, was in surprisingly good condition at the
end of my stay. I always carried a knife in my belt, and never wore sunglasses
because I wasn't allowed any.*

Bhutan, Kingdom of The Thunder Dragon

Following in my grand-parents' footsteps, my cousin Maybe and I trekked across Bhutan in 1995, using maps, diaries and drawings of the country that had been all but closed to the outside world until 1930. In January of that year, my grandfather had been deputed to travel from Sikkim via Tibet into the landlocked Kingdom of the Thunder Dragon to confer upon the King of Bhutan the KCIE, the order of Knight Commander of the Indian Empire, as a mark of respect and friendship from the government of Great Britain. The King had asked that the ceremony should take place in Bumthang, a long march from the western pass over which my grandfather's retinue had crossed. It was mid-winter: they were met by bare-foot soldiers in splendid apparel, and they walked and rode for three weeks through the snowy mountains, resting at night in gorgeous silk-clad tents with braziers inside and orange trees in blossom outside, all prepared on orders from the King. With pack ponies and yaks, and carrying enough china and silver to throw banquets for their hosts, Grandpa Weir's expedition numbered about a hundred, with Granny's dogs coming

In Bhutan, a country the size of Switzerland, there are only six hundred thousand people or so; Maybe and I could stare for miles without seeing any sign of human life.

Left: Grandpa Weir in the uniform of the Fifth Cavalry.

Below: The Weir contingent on their journey; they were greeted by splendidly-clad musicians and warriors with bare feet.

Above: my grandparents sit on either side of His Majesty, with my young Aunt Joan Mary behind Grandpa. Prayer flags in the background.

Left: after the ceremony the King and Queen of Bhutan posed for a formal photograph.

along for the ride; my seventeen–year-old aunt, Joan Mary travelled with them, equipped with her drawing things as she and Granny were accomplished artists. (My 10-year-old mother Beatrice was at school in England; she felt envious of this great adventure.) Unlike my grandparents, Maybe and I would make use of new roads and jeeps and waterproof tents for part of the journey: but we would have the luxury of sleeping in guesthouses and small hotels as well.

How much would the country have changed in sixty-five years? Well, there was an airport to start with, a small airstrip with a gaily painted building surrounded by mountains crowded in so close that you had to have special skills to land without smashing the wings of the aircraft against the steeply wooded hills. We went in October when the leaves were turning gold and smoke rose from village fires in slim straight plumes. Everywhere we heard the snap of prayer-flags, as this Buddhist country went about its daily round combining the tenets of the faith into all they did. The dzongs, monasteries crossed with administrative centres, hummed with deep-throated chanting, while the streets were buzzing with schoolchildren who had never seen television or played Gameboy. We camped in the high hills, and woke to find the tents and the porters' dogs white with frost; we washed our socks in streams and compared our trip with the notes and maps that my grandfather had made. When we arrived at our destination, it was resonant with ghosts of those long gone; afternoon sunlight slanted on to the floor of the shrine where the ceremony had taken place and dust mixed with smoke from butter lamps under the benevolent gaze of huge Buddhas half hidden in darkness. There had been an enormous feast prepared in the meadow outside the temple after the honour had been conferred, and all were invited, villagers and nobles alike. There had been archery and dancing: as we stood on the sunny grass we could almost hear the voices and the laughter, echoing down the years.

When it was time for their departure, the King came with my grandparents to the wild hills, to the very border, to say farewell in person: he and my grandfather had become close friends in a short space of time. Presents were exchanged: on the list of British gifts, we noted that among the cloth and china was a trunk full of rifles. Bhutan still holds a strategically sensitive and important place between the great powers of China and India. She is still independent; long may she remain so.

A touching farewell between two friends: Grandpa receives a ceremonial silk scarf from His Majesty.

Grandpa Weir could speak many languages fluently. While he was in Tibet, he studied Tibetan Buddhism and became something of an expert on the religion: much of his time was spent with the 13th Dalai Lama, as his duties and position put him in line to assist Tibet with the encroaching threat of a Chinese invasion. As spiritual and political head of Tibet, the Dalai Lama was an enormously important figure as well as being regarded as a god by his followers. A great and warm friendship sprang up between the two men and again many presents were exchanged. Our family homes are full of thangkas (religious wall hangings), teapots, statues and carvings from Tibet, Sikkim and Bhutan.

Our pack animals wind their way towards our next campsite. The high clean air and snow-capped mountains made our spirits soar. Sometimes we rode, but mostly walked.

The covered bridge at
Paro hasn't changed from
the time my grandparents
crossed it.

Far up on the sheer
rocky hillside hangs the
Tiger's Nest monastery,
Taktsang.

231

*Stupendously grand, and
painted in colours of strength
and simplicity, I think the
Tashicho Dzong's architecture
is as fine as I've ever seen.
There is an air of cheerful
purpose in the courtyard as
monks and townspeople go
about their business.*

The Dalai Lama

When I had the invitation to go to Dharamsala to interview the 14th Dalai Lama about his forthcoming trip to Britain, my mother asked me to take one of the most treasured pieces in our collection: a wooden-ended book containing a scripture, a story of a saint, hand-written years before, and presented by the 13th Dalai Lama to Grandpa. In the Chinese invasion of Tibet in 1950, almost all the monasteries had been sacked and burned to the ground, with all their holy manuscripts

Meeting the Dalai Lama in Dharamsala, and giving him the scripture his predecessor had given to my grandfather. The wooden covers of the book were made in Nepal.

Opposite: a beautiful thangka of the Green Tara painted for me by Sarika Singh.

Now exiled from Tibet, the 14th Dalai Lama tours the world speaking peace. Here, in Oxford, he is holding a picture of Granny Weir and a Tibetan noblewoman taken in 1929; Maybe and I often go to hear his lectures.

Opposite: The 13th Dalai Lama on his throne in the Potala Palace, Lhasa, photographed by my grandfather.

With the Dalai Lama and Sir Bernard Wetherill at the House of Commons, to draw attention to the plight of Tibet. The world continues to sit on its hands.

destroyed; monks, nuns and citizens were killed in their hundreds of thousands as the country was crushed by China's superior forces, watched in silence by the rest of the world. My mother wanted His Holiness to have one treasure at least, made even more important by its provenance. So I wrapped it carefully, tied it with silk ribbon and upon my arrival in Dharamsala, the Indian home of the Tibetan Government in exile, I humbly presented it to His Holiness, saying it came with affection and sympathetic support from my family. The Dalai Lama exclaimed with delight, studied the text closely, going 'Hmmm…hmmmm…ah good…' He took the text in his hands and put aside the cover. Then he summoned a young monk and whispered to him. The monk left the room and our talk continued, far beyond the fifteen minutes we had been allocated. Just before we took our leave, the monk returned with a scripture, and, bowing low, gave it to the Dalai Lama. He gave back to me the two carved wooden book-ends ('Old, valuable … you keep these') and replaced the original text with another, far older one ('Sniff! This smells old, bad smell!' followed by roars of laughter). Suddenly serious, he said that it was a treatise on Emptiness, the highest attainment a Buddhist can reach, and that it was for my family with his thanks and love.

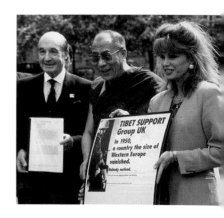

237

Indonesia and the Person in the Jungle

Anything that concerns the natural world concerns us all. If creatures become extinct because of man's behaviour I don't think we will be easily forgiven by the generations who come after us, let alone the creatures themselves. (Remember what that Greek philosopher said: 'If horses could draw, they would draw horses as gods'. We may yet have got it wrong.) It's not as if we don't know what's happening. The programme *Last Chance to Save...* invited me to Indonesia to see what was being done to try to save the Person of the Jungle , the orangutan, from certain oblivion. These tall distinguished apes lead a solitary existence, bearing one baby once every three or four years, hunting alone for fruit in the canopies of the rain forests, shy, powerful but no match for Man who is busy destroying every vestige of the habitat the apes need to survive. Loggers and the exploding population mean that there is an on-going struggle for territory, with the apes coming out as losers every time. The mothers are killed and the young apes are sold as pets. As they outgrow their cruel enclosures, some manacled to beds or hammered into crates, they become violent as a teenager would (and they grow at the same speed as humans; we are so like them it makes you gasp).

Jamie took this picture of the great red ape and me: orang-utans share many characteristics with humans, one of them being the ability to sit quietly in the grass thinking of not very much.

Primatologist Biruté Galdikas lived with the orangutans for years. She adopted the most vulnerable babies, who have to be taught to climb and eat and find food, just as our children have to be taught. There is a programme to re-habilitate the animals when they are able to fend for themselves, but thick and fast arrive more babies, wide-eyed and traumatised, clinging to any kind arms, helpless and stunned by their mother's death. The orangutans I met were fascinating; I was led into the jungle by one young ape with a baby of her own to look for her naughty little son, who wouldn't come when she called and when he did got a clout to discipline him. I watched an ape pretending to hammer nails into a plank of wood, carefully taking imaginary tacks from his pursed lips, watching slyly for our approval. We took three apes to be released and were greeted by the frankly terrifying sight of the wild orangutans swinging out of the jungle to meet the newcomers. (I saw an angry ape push a tree down with a sharp shove; you don't mess with these chaps.) The thought of a world without these giants is intolerable, and yet the clock is ticking, ticking, and the huge trees of the last rainforests on earth are crashing down as I write. What are we going to do? And more importantly, when are we going to do it?

The tiny tents in the Nubian Desert just allowed you to stretch out full-length. I apply make-up as though I am going shopping in Bond Street, i.e. lavishly, and why not.

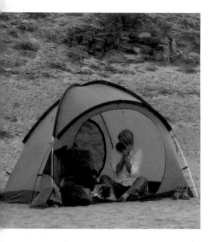

Journey to the Source of the Nile

The only major river in the world to flow from south to north is the Nile. The location of its source remained a mystery until the middle of the 19th century. I had been on the Nile in Egypt, but would I like to trace the mighty river back to its source? Travelling through Egypt, the Sudan, Ethiopia, Uganda and Rwanda? You bet.

The best way to film documentaries is with a tiny crew so we set out on this long adventure with two cameramen, a sound recordist, a producer, a medic as we would be off the beaten track for much of the time, and me. At each stage of the journey we linked up with an interpreter, our fixer, who knew the country, could translate for us and get us out of scrapes. We made friends with a camel called Charley Brown, camped in the Nubian desert, followed crocodiles and scrambled up mountains. We panted along behind the Simien Girl Runners at ten thousand feet in Ethiopia and nearly melted in underground burial chambers in Sudan. I was baptised Child of the Righteous on the Blue Nile, and given fresh goat's milk yoghurt to

Matt directs the cameraman Will and sound recordist Kiff as we ride towards the pyramids. I am in the middle on Charley Brown, the gentle camel whose whiskery kisses and cloud-soft footsteps made him my friend for life.

drink by a nomad. In Uganda, surrounded by hippos, we watched the sun set on elephants wading in the shallows of this immense and thrilling river. The wind blows from the north, assisting boats upstream (and down the map); then the tide brings them downstream again, flowing forever towards the Mediterranean, bringing its vast and vital waters to the hungry earth on its banks through five countries.

On the last day of our long tough journey we found we had to hack through thick Rwandan jungle, south of the Equator, and there finally at the end of our quest was a teeny, tiny trickle of spring water oozing quietly in the mud. I knelt down and collected some in a miniature gin bottle (amazing how old habits die hard) and marked on the label the date and what it was: Water from the Source of the Nile. It is kept in our bedroom, beside my model of Maudeline Everglot from Corpse Bride given to me by Tim Burton (see page 170).

The hospitality of people who have very little is always touching; in this nomadic shelter a sweet pipe tootles and the hardships of the world are forgotten.

The skiddoos took a while to get used to and then there was no stopping me.

Ice formed on our eye-lashes and balaclavas, as with the wind-chill factored in it was minus 50 degrees before dawn.

To the Land of Northern Lights

When I was growing up in Malaya I had a book called Ponny the Penguin; in it was a drawing of the night sky with what looked like a silk curtain fluttering in the blackness. Little Ponny gazed up at in awe; I wanted more than anything to see that eerie and astonishing sight with my own eyes. The Aurora can be seen in the Arctic and Antarctic, caused by the solar winds which speed past our planet Earth to be sucked back by our magnetic fields.

Our plan was to travel to the arctic circle in March, when night and day are equal as the endless midnight of winter turns to endless day in mid-summer. We travelled by train and dog sled, plane, car and boat, crossing snowy wastes and choppy seas, feverishly searching for the Northern Lights in the short time our budget would allow. Every time we stopped we asked: Will we see them here? And, time after time, a slow shaking of the head; it was too warm, too cold, too cloudy to see the Tricky Lady, as the Aurora is called in Norway. We slept in an ice-hotel, and rode skiddoos with reindeer running alongside; we watched from fishermens' huts, and drove on roads whose surfaces were deep in ice… but not a trace was to be seen. Then we had the good fortune to meet Kjetil Skogli, whose whole life is dedicated to chasing the

Aurora. He had developed a sixth sense about when this phenomenon would show itself; and just as we were beginning to lose hope he suddenly said: 'Pack the cars, we go. We shall drive like mad and we shall see the Lights an hour and a half from here. But hurry; tonight is the night.' Clad in every layer of clothing you can imagine and some you can't, we sped off round the fjords as the evening darkened the sky, to a lonely shore facing north. Stuffing ourselves into survival suits, for you can freeze to death in minutes in the Arctic if you aren't well prepared, we stood on the snowy beach and stared at the heavens.

The dogs loved to run, and howled when they had to stop. They preferred cold to the warmth of a hut, rolling in the snow and eating it in mouthfuls.

My pink pixie hat was given to me, with mittens, useful in the chilly splendour of the ice-hotel. The fire is fake. It was as cold as a tomb.

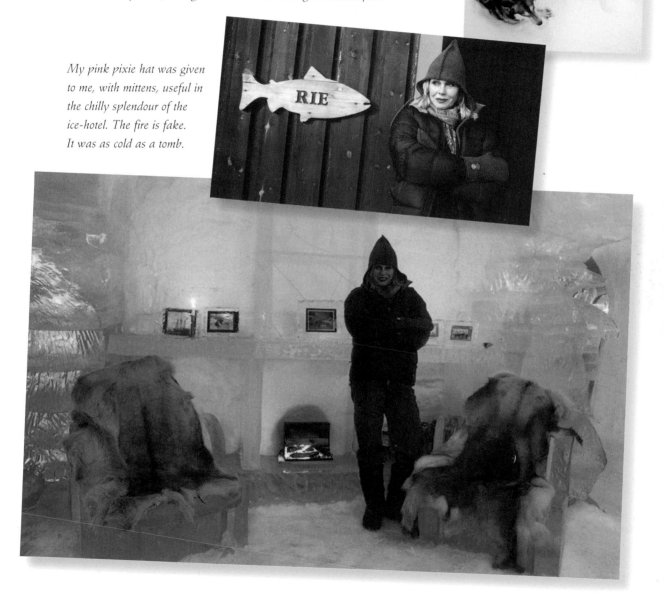

Opposite: the silk curtain of the Aurora Borealis, indescribably thrilling to see with your own eyes.

Trying to stand without moving in a strong wind to be filmed with the Tricky Lady. We had ice boots and survival suits or I wouldn't be writing this.

Nothing: then… something! A green billowing in the sky, a flurry of what looked like harp strings, a soft explosion of crimson, like a firework in slow motion and the show began.

I'm not sure how long it lasted: two, three hours? I seemed not to be cold any more, wanted to lie on my back to stare at the whole sky, as the lights flicked and blazed across the inky blackness and the moon and stars could be seen shining serenely behind it all. I remember trying to stand still in the fierce wind so that the camera could catch me and the Aurora together; but their light is so strange that normal film cameras can't catch their colour, so you have to shoot at 10 frames a second, and then dilute the colour later because it becomes saturated… I know nothing of the mechanics of how we captured them: I only know we did, and for a moment I felt, for the first time in my life, as if I was in the universe itself and that all will be well. Whatever happens after this, I thought, all will be well.

My Family

I often drew Jamie; he was patient up to a point but sometimes demanded more money. He looks a bit like me but more like his father Michael, who took this picture of him looking immensely cool and James Dean-ish.

The most extraordinary thing about children is the speed at which they grow: it seems that only moments elapse between tidying up toy soldiers one day and being picked up in a car driven by your child the next. Now Jamie towers over me and when I get into the car he usually has his wife and our two granddaughters inside. I have often thought that time goes in splodges, not a straight line: at this minute I still feel as though I am in the same splodge as when I was drawing Jamie wearing my safari hat, having paid him the princely sum of 10p an hour; my mind is the same, although circumstances are now entirely different (he would now charge far more: two quid at least). But if I glance in the mirror I see what Alice and Emily would see: their grandmother, with a shade too much make-up round the eyes, hair dyed yellow, looking a hundred and grinning like a Cheshire cat. They won't ever see the Me that I still think I am, forever aged thirty, with abundant energy and hungry for work. (The next splodge, coming soon I expect, will be the last one, and may last for ages; a plateau to take me from here to eternity, with a lavender rinse in my thinning hair.)

Looking back through a photograph collection is frankly awe-inspiring: why did I wear that dress, was I really that fat/thin/frizzy/boring, look at that necklace, who is the fellow on the left … but the truth is I can remember all of these things with clarity as though it were yesterday, as though it were now. Time rolls on: and just as we begin to get the gist of the riddle the train blows its whistle and it's all aboard.

I wouldn't have been able to cope with Jamie's upbringing without my parents. They were always there, to have us to stay during his school holidays, to

At a photo-shoot with Jamie, when he was very small and rather
bored by the slow proceedings. Indian bedspread dress in evidence; it
was still the sixties.

look after the boy while I was filming abroad: to help me out and pick me up and provide a home from home for us both. They were parents beyond worth, and Jamie and I are always eternally grateful for what they did for us. Being a single parent is difficult largely because of logistics; how to get back from the studios in time to collect your son from Cubs; what to do when all the filming dates change during half-term: where to turn to for a loan when the banks won't let you in. We muddle on by, men as well as women, half bread-winner, half home-maker, and things which are problems can be sorted out with time and sympathy on your side. I loved having Jamie with me on shoots and trips abroad: he came with me to Canada and France, Australia, Switzerland, Italy, Mauritius, America and Greece. His father's family were rock solid for him as well; and Michael's early influence on him has resulted in Jamie following in his footsteps and becoming a photographer too. How lucky we are to be so fond of each other; and so proud, too, that we all belong together as a family: an extended, elongated, slightly unorthodox and therefore completely normal family.

Jamie was fascinated by cameras from an early age; here he examines Michael's Pentax with an amateur's keen eye.

Above: we have both tidied ourselves up for this picture taken by Patrick Lichfield at his London studio in Aubrey Walk. Right: Patrick and Jamie both went to Harrow School; the Harrow hat is worn at an angle over the face.

My father had 'joined the majority', (his favourite phrase for dying) before Jamie and Tessa met and married. Alice, their eldest daughter, was brought to meet her great-grandmother when my mother had moved into a small cottage in Rolvenden where I grew up. That soft summer afternoon Tessa took a picture of four generations of Lumleys: Alice will look at it when she is old, and see how time stretches forwards and backwards at the same time.

Jamie shot past me in height; my hair is dyed black for Vanilla *and my role as Miralda Sumac. He was still at school.*

Jamie and Tessa in Scotland. She can beat anyone at Scrabble, but I am the one who does the hair-cutting in the family.

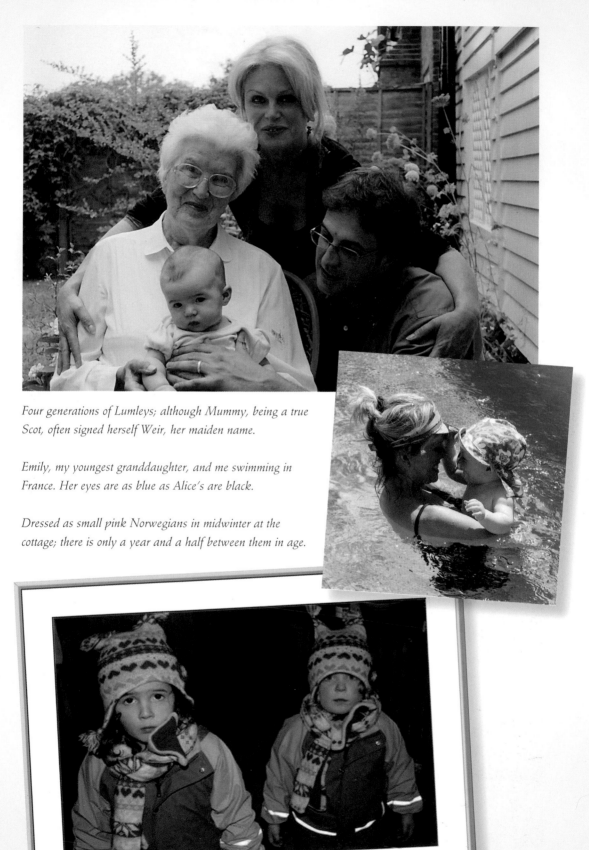

Four generations of Lumleys; although Mummy, being a true
Scot, often signed herself Weir, her maiden name.

Emily, my youngest granddaughter, and me swimming in
France. Her eyes are as blue as Alice's are black.

Dressed as small pink Norwegians in midwinter at the
cottage; there is only a year and a half between them in age.

Above right: I carry this polaroid picture of Stevie with me wherever I go. I wish I could sing well; we look as though we have been trying out some Noel Coward songs at the piano in Wimbledon.

Right: what would it be like, I wonder, to read a music score like a book and hear every note of the whole orchestra? Stephen knows, and thinks it's completely normal. I am in awe.

I first nearly met Stephen Barlow when he was thirteen and due to come out to lunch with the son of friends of mine. (I was 21, and had already had Jamie.) The boy Barlow, by all accounts staggeringly musical and rather tricky, never arrived and I can remember thinking: 'Bother: I would have liked to meet that black-haired difficult boy.' Ten years passed, and my friends' son got married; and playing the organ at his wedding was black-haired, difficult Stephen Barlow. (When I set eyes on him I felt as though I had been given an electric shock.) We talked, exchanged addresses, nothing more as we were both tied up with other people. Eight years after that meeting I had a message out of the blue: he was rehearsing nearby, could he drop in for tea. And so our life together began, completely unplanned and unexpected, and continues to this day; soon we will have been married for twenty-five years. Do I believe in love at first sight, in fate, in luck? I do, I absolutely do.

We have lived in Wimbledon, where we ran out of money trying to buy a house beyond our means, in Kent in a marvellous and rather rickety parsonage, and in London where we hear Big Ben striking the hour and foxes yowling in the night. We bought a tumbledown ruin of a cottage in Scotland and restored it, bringing in spring water from the hills and planting trees where there had been none. Owls and bats and

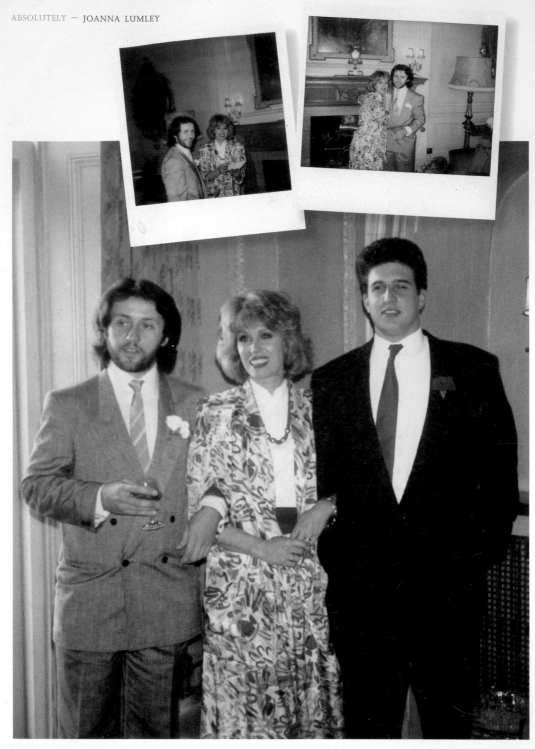

When we got married at Fort William it was a very small affair; only our immediate families came, and Jamie was Best Man. I wore a summery suit I already had, and bought a bunch of flowers at a petrol station on the way to the register office. Our wedding lunch at the Inverlochy Castle Hotel afterwards was wonderful and discreet beyond words.

Sometimes I make Stevie do non-conductorish things like carry a bear to a Teddy Bear Fair in aid of charity. As a musician he is able to take the rough with the smooth: but actually we were both delighted to be there.

He shall have music

Stephen Barlow, 16, of the King's School, Canterbury, has become an associate of the Royal College of Organists. He used to be a Canterbury Cathedral chorister.

A 16-year-old pupil at King's School and a former Canterbury Cathedral chorister has become an Associate of the Royal College of Organists after studying the organ for three years.

He is Stephen Barlow who entered the College diploma examinations earlier this month and on Saturday went to London to receive his certificate. He was also awarded the Sawyer prize for gaining second highest marks in organ playing.

Stephen trained for his diploma in a final concentrated study of four months under the tuition of cathedral organist and choirmaster, Mr. Allan Wicks.

The organ is now his favourite musical instrument, but he started learning the piano at the age of six and reached an advanced grade. He did not play the organ at all until becoming a pupil at King's.

Stephen said organ playing for him was a matter of experience. The technique was not so drastically different from the piano, apart from learning to use the pedals.

Seven King's School boys were successful in the December auditions for the National Youth Orchestra. Stephen was among them, playing percussion. He has also learned to play the tympani at King's.

Stephen is currently studying for "A" levels in music, English and history. He hopes to get an organ scholarship to Cambridge University in the future.

Composing is another part of Stephen's musical interest. In 1967 Canterbury Cathedral choir sang his arrangement for the Magnificat and Nunc Dimittis.

He said: "In fact I write a tremendous amount of music, but only about half of it is at all serviceable."

Before joining Canterbury Cathedral Choir School Stephen was a chorister at Chelmsford Cathedral. He is also a member of the King's School choir.

This year he is working towards becoming a Fellow of the Royal College of Organists, which will take him one step nearer his ambition of being a cathedral organist and choirmaster.

However, Stephen's life is not all music. He would like to devote more time to sport, especially cricket. He is also grateful to his music instructors, Mr. Wicks and Mr. Edred Wright, director of music at King's, who has given him great encouragement.

A FLIGHT OF THREE?

The average person's reaction to the arctic climate is one big shiver, but for 20-year-old Ursula Brown, of Montfort Close, Canterbury, surviving in the arctic is part of her training in the Women's Royal Air Force.

Ursula, a senior aircraftwoman, left England on

took the idea to heart and Mrs. Brown said that both her daughters are very happy.

Ursula is based at R.A.F. Northolt, Middlesex, and Barbara at High Wickham in Buckinghamshire. But the Brown family could make it a flight of three. Mrs. Brown's youngest daughter, Julia, 14, is also a pupil at St. Anselm's. She is leaving school later in the year and one of her ideas is to join the W.R.A.F.

PUBLIC   **"Burns Night"**

Soft machine

Stephen was made a Fellow of the Royal College of Organists at the age of sixteen. He has conducted orchestras all over the world, plays the piano and organ like a fiend and composes music into the bargain. I am sometimes allowed to turn the pages but am largely out of my depth.

Far right, above: listening to him playing in the Music Room, Alice became transfixed, holding her hand out like a tiny dalek to collect all the notes she heard.

Far right, below: I love watching an orchestra in full flight and never more than when Stevie is conducting. The Albanian Opera Orchestra played up a storm; musicians are the business.

Absolutely fabulous news for opera lovers

By Neil Johnston
Arts Correspondent

A FAMOUS conductor and his absolutely fabulous wife were in Belfast today — to go to a party.

He is Stephen Barlow, who is the new artistic director of Opera Northern Ireland.

And she is the glamorous stage and screen star, Joanna Lumley.

The couple were here for a reception to mark the company's 10th anniversary and to introduce Stephen to the media.

His new appointment means he will be spending up to five months in the province every year.

Although the couple need somewhere to live, Stephen dispelled widespread rumours that they have already found an Ulster home.

"We are still house hunting. But we now have a pretty good idea of what we want — somewhere in the inner city where I will not be out of touch.

"There is no real hurry because I won't be coming over regularly until early spring."

Joanna will be accompanying her husband to Belfast as often as her acting commitments allow.

"We are both looking forward to it very much," said Stephen. "We plan to do a bit of entertaining when we are here."

At today's reception, Opera Northern Ireland announced their plans for the future, which includes a major corporate membership scheme aimed at getting more financial backing for opera from the business community.

● See page 5

High fliers: Stephen Barlow with his wife, Joanna Lumley, on their arrival at Belfast International Airport.

Picture by Roy Smyth.

Right: painstakingly restoring the cottage: the roof needed stripping right back but we used all the Welsh slates again. A kitchen wing was added, nestling into the hillside, a farm track was made and meadow flowers planted.

Above: by the time we had added the fire circle I knew we were in paradise. Alice and Emily, ready as ever to make a bonfire, like it as much as we do.

stoats live with us there, small birds join their song with the curlews and buzzards wheeling above the valleys, and if we are lucky we get snowed in and have to live by candlelight during power cuts. Jamie, Tessa and the girls come up to stay and I think that nothing could be better than sitting watching the sunset from the fire circle, with supper cooking inside and the meadow flowers waist high around us. Dear cottage: if we hadn't have saved it when we did, it would have fallen down stone by stone until there was nothing left. Instead we can walk out onto the dewy grass at midnight and see the huge black sky silent above us, studded with stars as bright as diamonds.

The Gurkhas

My father Jimmy Lumley at the battle of Mogaung; the Chindits operated at the centre of the grim conflict in Burma.

In the Second World War, General Orde Wingate's Chindits were formed to operate behind enemy lines in Burma: Japan's army had swept down through the country forcing the British forces back into India. The Chindits were dropped by air, with mules, at night on secretly prepared landing strips; they operated in small units and the fighting was bloody and awful. Gurkha regiments, including my father's, the 6th Gurkha Rifles, contributed many men to these secretive and lethal brigades, named after the Chinthe, a mythical animal which guarded the Burmese temples. It was during the assault on Mogaung that Rifleman Tul Bahadur Pun was awarded the VC for his heroic and selfless action; the horrifying battle saw many casualties, one of whom was my father's best friend, Michael Allmand, who was also awarded a VC, but posthumously. My father wouldn't talk of those dark days; if we could get anything out of him it would be stories of the Gurkhas' outstanding courage, their love of fun and unwavering loyalty. When I was six my father showed me a photograph of Tul Bahadur Pun VC and said: 'That's one of the bravest men you will ever see.'

In 2008 I got a call out of the blue from a man called Peter Carroll. As a Folkestone councillor he was coming across many stories of hardship in his community of retired Gurkha soldiers who had come to Britain hoping to find work. Commonwealth soldiers who had served four years were allowed to apply for the right to reside and the right to become British citizens, but Nepal, where the Gurkhas come from, had never been part of the Commonwealth so this law didn't apply to them. Many were too poor to fly home: they received no social services (and they didn't want them) and were not permitted to work, which was their only goal. To work in the country they loved second only to their own, to bring up their children with a good

260

With the two loyal VCs who were at the front of our campaign: Lacchiman Gurung and Tul Bahadur Pun. Their actions which earned them their deserved medals were brave beyond belief. The Victoria Cross, awarded for conspicuous gallantry, is worn nearest to the centre of the chest on a red ribbon.

261

Opposite: After the photograph appeared of me brandishing an unsheathed kukri, the famous curved Gurkha knife, an indignant man wrote to complain that I was carrying a dangerous weapon and should be prosecuted. The police used to say that you didn't need any security whatsoever during our rallies, as they were full of the most effective soldiers on earth.

education and to serve the Queen in whatever way they could…that was their aim. They didn't want charity: they wanted justice.

Peter Carroll and the law firm, Howe and Co, had submitted six test cases to the High Court of five Gurkha veterans and a Gurkha widow. Was it fair that men who had been prepared to die for our country were not allowed to live here? Would I help to publicise the cause? Could we get the British public behind us? Then started one of the most extraordinary and challenging campaigns imaginable. I can only write the barest bones of the proceedings: how we met, in cafes and doorways to discuss strategies, often emailing each other in the early hours of the morning; how all of us, engaged full-time in our 'day jobs', decided that, come hell or high water, we would never give in until we got the fair deal we were seeking; that Gurkhas should be treated like their Commonwealth counterparts. Martin Howe, David Enright and Kieran O'Rourke, the three lawyers who had prepared the case for the High Court, were indefatigable. Without Legal Aid no Gurkha would have been able to approach a lawyer; Legal Aid was vital, for without representation there can be no justice. More often than not it was just us five at the forefront, Peter, Martin, David, Kieran and me, attending enquiries, writing letters, rallying the

Mr Brown took all the cartoons in good humour; when he took up the reins from the Home Office, things moved at breakneck speed.

Overleaf: The press and media support was invaluable: by keeping our cause in high profile they put relentless pressure on the Government.

JOANNA GETS AN AB FAB RESULT
Joanna Lumley has won her campaign to secure settlement rights for Gurkhas. The actress, 63, whose father served with the feared soldiers, met PM Gordon Brown in Downing Street this morning ahead of the official announcement by Home Secretary Jacqui Smith. BROWN U-TURN: P4

Guardian profile Joanna Lumley

> Her passion for the Gurkhas' cause has been tireless, it has known no bounds. She is a true honour to her father

High court ruling means a national treasure will be staying in Britain after all

THE SUNDAY POST/ June

Joanna Lumley's praise for generous Sunday Post readers

You're just Absolutely Fabulous!

By Paul Johnson

GAESO

Joanna praised the generosity of our readers

Daily Mail

DAILY NEWSPAPER OF THE YEAR 50p

ABSOLUTELY FARCICAL!

Joanna Lumley ambushes hapless minister over Gurkhas ... and dictates government policy to him

SEE PAGES 8 AND 9

ABSOLUTELY OUTRAGEOUS

Act

4 **NEWS**

Chaos reigns as Lumley leads Brown a merry dance

▶ Actress meets with immigration minister over contradictory letters

Gurkhas aim to get action

FOR VETERANS

GURKHA JUSTICE

Saved by my £15 Halfords helmet

Gurkish delight

JOANNA'S JOY AS HEROES CAN STAY

Now peers back Gurkhas' battle to stay in Britain

Lumley to go down in the history books

DAILY EXPRESS

GURKHAS STILL NEED YOUR HELP

Page 8 ＊＊   Daily Mail, Friday, May 8

Patsy puts min

Joanna Lumley dictates policy in the fight for Gurkhas' rights

By **Vanessa Allen, Ian Drury**
and **Matthew Hickley**

JOANNA Lumley staged an extraordinary ambush on Gordon Brown's hapless Immigration Minister over the Gurkhas yesterday.

In a bravura performance, the actress seized the initiative in her battle for soldiers' rights and reduced Phil Woolas to an abject and humiliated figure.

Adopting the air of an angry schoolmistress, she sought him out at Westminster and frogmarched him to a live press conference for a very public dressing down.

In the process, she effectively rewrote government policy. She was stung into action after two

Falklands War heroes received letters suggesting they were being barred from Britain – less than 24 hours after Gordon Brown had assured her that he would take personal charge of the Gurkhas' legal battle for citizenship rights.

In extraordinary scenes Miss Lumley – the daughter of a British Gurkha officer – signalled she was about to denounce the Government

for its betrayal of the veterans. The actress, best-known as Patsy in the comedy Absolutely Fabulous, and the minister ended up shoulder-to-shoulder after she outflanked Mr Woolas on the steps of a meeting, confronting him publicly over the shambles.

She pounced on the unwitting minister, announcing in her inimitable cut-glass tones: 'I want to speak to you.'

After emergency talks, the red-faced Immigration Minister was forced to insist the verdict on the veterans was an 'interim' one – and to suggest they would be allowed to stay after all.

The row centres on the immigration status of Gurkha veterans who retired before 1997. Rules introduced by Mr [Woolas] last month were fiercely criticised by campaigners, who warned [they] would place massive restrictions [on the] number of heroes admitted by [the country] they fought for.

[Last] week, Mr Brown suffered his [first Commons] defeat on the issue in [a vote] engineered by Liberal Democrat [leader] Nick Clegg.

[Alt]hough the result was not binding [up]on the Government, ministers

insisted they would revise immigration rules by July and fast-track 1,500 outstanding immigration applications from Gurkha veterans.

Yesterday campaigners were furious to learn that despite Mr Brown's assurances, a number of veterans had received letters saying they could not stay in Britain under existing rules.

Mr Woolas attempted to insist that the letters had not really rejected the men's cases, saying: 'This is not a letter of rejection, it's a letter of explanation.'

Miss Lumley raised an elegant eyebrow before telling the hapless minister what he was really trying to say. She said: 'The minister has explained, and I think we are agreed, that we are going to be able to help in the formulation of new guidelines. That is wonderful.'

Embarrassingly for the Government, Miss Lumley said Downing Street had appeared surprised by the letters. She said an official phoned to beg her to postpone her planned press conference.

She told Mr Woolas: 'Downing Street telephoned me and said, "We have just heard about these letters", Gordon Brown didn't know about them.

'It seemed that the Prime Minister didn't know about them and I think he was very anxious because it is in direct contradiction of what we were talking about yesterday... There seems to be, if I may say Mr Woolas, a gap in communication.'

The minister insisted the UK Border Agency – which considers residency applications – would recon-

Tearful Lumley 'ashamed' at Gurkha snub

●CAMPAIGNERS condemned new rules giving more ex-Gurkhas the right to live in Britain as a "disgrace" today. Immigration Minister Phil Woolas said the changes would allow about 4,300 more to settle here out of the 36,000 who served in the British Army before July 1997. But Gurkhas' supporters attacked the new criteria as "unattainable". One change means they don't qualify if they haven't served 20 years. Tearful campaigner Joanna Lumley she said she felt "ashamed".

Upset: actress Joanna Lumley today with an ex-Gurkha

Home Office
UK Border Agency

SETTLEMENT IN THE UNITED KINGDOM: IMMIGRATION DISCRETIONS FOR FORMER BRIGADE OF GURKHA MEMBERS

WHAT IS CHANGING AND WHEN?

From 24 April 2009 new criteria will be used to consider applications to settle in the United Kingdom outside of United Kingdom Immigration Rules from former members of the Brigade of Gurkhas (the Brigade).

WHY ARE CHANGES BEING MADE?

The High Court in the United Kingdom ruled that the previous guidance was unclear and did not adequately reflect factors relating to length and quality of service in the Brigade.

WHAT ARE THE NEW DISCRETIONARY CRITERIA?

Permission to settle in the United Kingdom may be granted if you meet <u>one</u> of the following:

- You spent at least three years continuous lawful residence in the United Kingdom during or after service;

- You have close family settled in the United Kingdom with whom you enjoy family life within the meaning of Article 8 of the European Convention on Human Rights (ECHR);

- You received a Level 1-3 Award[1] for gallantry, leadership or bravery for service in the Brigade;

- You completed 20 or more years' service in the Brigade;

- You have a chronic/long term medical condition which is attributable to, or was aggravated by, service in the Brigade.

If you do not qualify under any of the above, permission to settle in the United Kingdom may also be granted if you meet any <u>two</u> of the following:

- You were previously awarded a United Kingdom Ministry of Defence disability pension, but no longer have a chronic/long term medical condition attributable to, or aggravated by, service in the Brigade;

- You received a Mention in Dispatches (Level 4 Award) for service in the Brigade;

[1] Level 1: Victoria Cross
Level 2: DSO/DCM, DSO/DCM Bar, IDSM (India Distinguished Service Medal)
Level 3: Military Cross, Military Cross Bar Military Medal, Military Medal Bar, Jangi Inam

The Guardian | Thu

News

Bro
nov

Labour rebe
blow to PM'

Vote is triu
attack on 'sh

Nicholas Watt a

Gordon Brown wa
shore up his auth
first Commons d
when MPs vote
Gurkhas to settle

Days after bei
his plans to refo
expenses and all
support of 27 La
the Liberal Dem

Up to 75 other
the vote, which
Gurkhas be allo
just those who
small proportio
Pound resigned
night after join

A few hours a
government wa
ment in which
Phil Woolas, an
to allay the ang
● The 1,300 Gu
on whether the
have their case
May, rather tha
● A governme
its policy will
published befor
● A Gurkha wh
settle in the U
sion implemen
of the review.
● Government
Friday will be

Mr Wool
request fo
rejected. A
that around 100 Gurkhas had
told in recent days that they wou
allowed to stay in Britain.

But the humiliating spectacle
seized upon by Opposition MP
another disaster for Mr Brown
his beleaguered Government.
failure of the Home Office to r
Downing Street of the letters wa
seen as another nail in the coffi
Home Secretary Jacqui Smith, w
facing the axe in a forthcoming
net reshuffle.

Tory leader David Cameron sa
think we are in a situation where
left hand of this Government do
know what the right hand is d

ly Mail, Friday, May 8, 2009

ster in his place

ruised after defeat over Gurkhas – the little matter of MPs' expenses

Joanna Lumley, David Cameron and Nick Clegg celebrate the parliamentary victory for the Gurkhas' right to settle in Britain Photograph: Shaun Curry/AFP/Getty Images

Cameron is attracted by the Young

You applied to settle in the United Kingdom on 31/10/2006 as a former Gurkha. Your application was refused because you were discharged from the British Army in Nepal before 1 July 1997 and you did not therefore meet the requirements of the relevant immigration rules (paragraph 276F)

Denied entry: The letter to Gyanendra Rai refusing him permission to live in Britain

The Prime Minister has absolutely got to get a grip on this issue and recognise that public opinion has spoken, Parliamentary opinion has spoken, and this issue needs to be sorted, and sorted out right now.'

LibDem home affairs spokesman Chris Huhne said: 'At worst this was a betrayal of the Gurkhas and at best a monumental shambles in Government where one part did-

n't know what the other part was doing.'

The letters sent to Gurkha veterans, from Entry Clearance Officer Chris Feist, said: 'I have carefully considered your case against the criteria and regret to inform you that you do not qualify for settlement under the current guidance.'

The letters – to Falklands heroes Gyanendra Rai and Deo Prakash

Limbu – contained a caveat that the Borders Agency would review its guidance by July and would reconsider then.

But shocked campaigners said they were still an 'unequivocal rejection' of two men who had risked their lives to serve this country.

The letters sent out yesterday were to three of the five test cases

who formed a landmark High Court case last year, in which the Home Office was told its old policy was unfair.

Letters were sent to Mr Rai, Mr Limbu and a Gurkha widow who had also asked for the right to live here. One applicant, Birendra Man Shrestha, is still waiting to learn his fate while the fifth, Bhim Prasad Gurung, died waiting for the new Home Office policy to be announced.

During Prime Minister's Questions on Wednesday, Mr Brown pledged to 'listen' to Parliament after the Commons defeat. MPs – including 27 Labour rebels – voted for all veteran warriors to be allowed to live in Britain.

Comment – Page 14
v.allen@dailymail.co.uk

Mr Limbu, now 49, was awarded the South Atlantic Medal for his part in the 1982 conflict and served in the Army for almost seven years.

His case meets one of the secondary list of the new criteria, because he was awarded a campaign medal, but his case is believed to have failed because he did not meet one of the other criteria – a Ministry of Defence disability pension or a Mention in Dispatches.

troops and talking to the press. Sir 'Union Jack' Hayward gave a sum of money to set up a fighting fund; everyone wanted to do their bit.

The High Court decreed that the ruling was unfair and that the Government should re-write the laws. Spirits were high but not for long. The Government took its time, more than took its time: our requests were denied, our letters went unanswered, the new law remained unwritten. We stepped up our campaign, with a website so that people could sign up their support for the Gurkha Justice Campaign and what started as a trickle quickly became a flood, a torrent of indignation and sympathy for our most valiant allies. (People, unasked, often sent donations, which I carefully banked in a new account: it was earmarked to be given to the Gurkha Welfare Trust when the battle was over.)

Why didn't I know of this inequality before? Well, I just didn't; and nor did most of the British public, and indeed the members of our armed forces. We took it for granted that successive Governments would honour the Military Covenant, and in our name look after all those who had served our nation in war and peace. The response from the public was overwhelming in its demands: it wanted justice for the ex-Gurkhas and they would back us to the hilt. The press began to take a keener interest in the cause; editorial comment was largely on our side in the national papers, broadcasters followed the progress of our press conferences and photocalls. Throughout this arduous and often exhausting period the Gurkha contingency was faultless, turning up smartly dressed at rallies in Parliament Square, respectfully laying wreaths at the Cenotaph, standing in puzzlement as setbacks were announced and yelling their war cry 'Ayo Gorkhali!' when the news was good. At the head of the column, as it were, two frail men, well into their eighties and too weak to walk, sat in dignified silence in their wheel chairs: Lacchiman Gurung VC and Tul Bahadur Pun VC. (I met Mr Pun for the first time in my life outside the High Court; I had brought for him the little silver figure of a Gurkha piper that my late father had loved. The old warrior put his hand on my head as I knelt by his side and said 'You are my daughter now.')

Documents which were beyond price to us: the agenda in the House of Commons when Clegg challenged the Home Office ruling, and the High Court judgement declaring that the Gurkhas had been unlawfully treated.

Throughout the campaign, people from all sides of the political arena emerged as staunch allies, chief among them Nick Clegg. There were Tory peers and Labour backbenchers, Shadow ministers and senior policemen, but also servicemen and the Hindu Council, coffee morning ladies and rough sleepers, school children, vicars and celebrities… everyone was in support. Would the Government finally capitulate and write a law that allowed the ex-Gurkhas to reside and work here after their service days were over?

The tide began to turn. Parliament threw out a new set of rules, too hastily prepared by the Home Office, which, incredibly, made it even

Letters from David Cameron and Nick Clegg to me,
and the draft of my second letter to the PM Gordon
Brown, which sadly drew no response. I was urging
the PM to seize the chance to act swiftly to gain
maximum Brownie points.

harder for Gurkha veterans to attain the stated criteria; Nick Clegg and David Cameron led the revolt, which received warm support from all sides of the House, especially from the back benches of the Labour party.

The end came on a sunny day, a day that could have been written by Enid Blyton. After more meetings and messages, chaotic interviews and speculation I was summoned to 10 Downing Street on May 23rd to meet the Prime Minister at breakfast time. Mr Brown's handshake was warm; I mustn't tell the press waiting outside what the decision was, he said, but I should be allowed to smile broadly. Massed in Parliament Square were the Gurkhas and well-wishers, with the police showing their support for the event by smiling from ear to ear; and stacked in front of them were the crowded cameras of the press and media. A transistor relayed to the hushed crowd what the Home Secretary was saying in Parliament: the Gurkhas would be allowed to stay! A yell, a roar went up, taxis hooted, bus passengers craned to see, cameras flashed, everybody hugged everybody else and we just stared into each others' faces and eyes…we had won. That afternoon the Prime Minister invited forty Gurkhas to have tea at Downing Street; and when a hundred and fifty appeared, the Downing Street police just waved them in with a grin. There were three cheers for the Prime Minister, cakes and biscuits were handed round, kisses flew and cameras clicked, and the bells of Westminster Abbey suddenly rang out; it may have been a practice session but I think it was the angels overhead, signalling that justice had been done.

There are wrinkles to be ironed out as more Gurkhas apply to settle here, in small numbers, it is true, but they are arriving in a country already beset with its own financial difficulties: Dhan Gurung, the first Gurkha to be elected a councillor in the UK, has set up the Gurkha Services Link, and the service charities, especially the Gurkha Welfare Trust, continue with their unfailing support and advice. When you are building a new house you have to pause from time to time to see that you are doing it right, that the roof won't fall in, that the windows can open and close. Our country is historically reliant on immigration, and by welcoming the brave men of Nepal who have made it their life's duty to protect us, we are doing the right thing.

Our thrilling tour of Nepal later that year, the splendid receptions we were given everywhere we went, the love and gratitude that poured towards us, and towards the people of Great Britain, has made this one of the proudest episodes of my life. It was life-altering: a helter-skelter of learning curves, a tribute to the power of justice and the sheer goodness of ordinary people, an astonishing David and Goliath story with a happy ending, in the knowledge that a great wrong had been righted.

Would I do it all again? Absolutely.

With the red powder of a tikka, the Hindu mark of respect, covering my forehead, and great crimson garlands of flowers draped round my shoulders I make slow and happy progress through crowds of Nepali well-wishers. Looking up, I saw Jamie with his camera.

For all the people with whom I have ever worked,
everywhere in the world, with love and gratitude.

Photo Credits

The publishers would like to thank the following sources for their kind permission to reproduce the photographs and illustrations in this book. Every effort has been made to contact copyright holders, but we would be happy to correct any errors or omissions in future editions (Author's Collection except where stated).

John Adriaan: 74 (above right); 75 (middle row middle). 84 (right); 85. David Appleby: 134; 137 (all); 138-9. Brian Aris: 75 (below left); 152; 153. Clive Arrowsmith: 50 (above). Michael Barrett: 57. BBC Photo Library: 5; 74 (below middle); 105 (below); 190 (above); 191; 230 (above). BBC Top Gear: 107 (above left and right). Neil Campbell-Sharp: 255. Michael Claydon: 83 (all); 249 (below right). Wubbo de Jong: 253. Duffy: 66 (right). Freemantle Media: 4. Getty Images: 8 (above); 76 (above left, above right and below right); 104; 234; 235 (above left and below); 261. Annette Green: 94-5. Dinah Hasler: 250 (below); John Haynes: 141; 146 (all); 147. ITV/Rex Features: 169 (all). Wolfgang Jankhe: 158 (below). Jean Kertesz: 82. Giles Keyte/Baby Cow Productions: 190 (below); Mike Lawn: 163. Lidbrooke: 78 (all); 79. Lichfield Archive: 69 (above left, middle below); 74 (below left); 75 (above middle, middle left); 128 (left and right); 249 (below left). Jamie Lumley: 239; 257 (above); 271. Tessa Lumley: 251 (all). David Magnus/Rex Features: 92. Sylvia McMillan: 43; 45 (above and below). Richard Mildenhall: 143 (below right). Ed Miller/Baby Cow Productions: 190 (above). David Montgomery: 64; 65 (below). Terry O'Neill: 129. Sam Peek: 249 (above). Brian J Ritchie/Baby Cow Productions: 191; 191. Howard Rogerson: 74 (below right). Tony Russell: 162 (inset). Jennifer Saunders: 194(all); 195 (right); 196. Julius Silver: 90 (below). Peter Smith: 80. Sally Soames: 198 (all). David Steen: 81 (above). Peter Tauber: 113 (below); 124 (above). Martha Wailes: 216; 218 (all); 219. Crispian Woodgate: 52; 53 (all).

First published in Great Britain in 2011; reprinted in 2015
by Weidenfeld & Nicolson

10 9 8 7 6 5 4 3 2

Text © Joanna Lumley 2011
Design and layout © Weidenfeld & Nicolson 2011

A CIP catalogue record for this book is available from the British Library.

ISBN: 978 0 297 86760 9

Design by carrstudio.co.uk
Special photography by Martin Norris – www.martin-norris.co.uk
Origination by Alta Image, London
Printed and bound in Italy by Printer Trento

Weidenfeld & Nicolson
The Orion Publishing Group Ltd
Carmelite House
50 Victoria Embankment
London EC4Y 0DZ

An Hachette UK Company

Endpapers: detail of a blanket from the Swat Valley in Northern Pakistan; Granny Weir bought a large number of these in the 1930s and they now adorn the houses of her grateful grandchildren.